Florentine EMBROIDERY

Florentine EMBROIDERY

BARBARA SNOOK

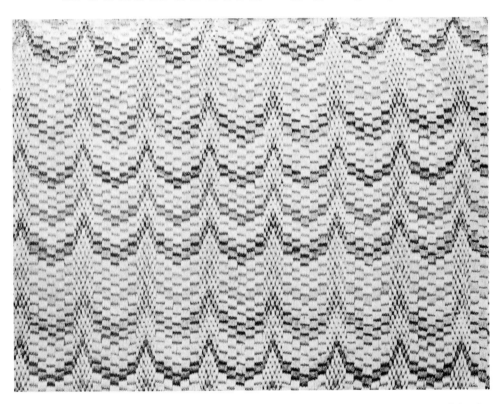

CHARLES SCRIBNER'S SONS · *New York*

PRINTED IN THE UNITED STATES OF AMERICA
SBN 684-10560-8
LIBRARY OF CONGRESS CATALOG CARD NUMBER 67-18133

CONTENTS

5

ACKNOWLEDGMENTS

My most grateful thanks are due to Mrs. Joan Toggitt for the initiative which provoked this book, and for her more recent help in checking availability of materials on both sides of the Atlantic; to the Embroiderers' Guild for the loan of collections and for early help and encouragement from Miss B. Sinclair Salmon, Miss de Denne and Mrs. N. Kimmins, and to Mr. Hilary Gardner, Librarian of the Embroiderers' Guild who devoted a considerable amount of time to helping in the initial stages of research.

Historical examples have been hard to discover and for a long while it seemed that only fragments remained, yet gradually, after following very slender clues, some magnificent examples have been found. I thank most gratefully His Grace the Duke of Buccleuch for permission to see the embroideries at Boughton House, Kettering, and Miss A. L. Kinnison for her help and detailed information about the upholstery; The Hon. Mrs. Clive Pearson for permission to examine and draw embroideries at Parham Park, Pulborough, and Miss Rosemary Courcier for her additional help; Colonel N. V. Stopford-Sackville, C.B.E., for permission to see the State Bed and a set of chairs at Drayton House, Lowick, Kettering; Mrs. P. A. Tritton who helped me find them; Miss Jean Alexander for permission to see the chairs at Aubrey House, and for the gift of one of the original pieces of upholstery; Mrs. Ramsay Harvey for the loan of Victorian samplers and use of the patterns; the staff of the Textile Department of the Victoria and Albert Museum; William Wells, Esq., Keeper of the Burrell Collection, City of Glasgow Museum and Art Gallery; The Hon. R. B. Kay-Shuttleworth, M.B.E., J.P., The Gawthrope Foundation; Mrs. G. Hamilton-King for permission to examine the samplers at the Royal School of Needlework; Professor Luciano Berti for information about the chairs in the Bargello, Florence.

To Miss Alice B. Beer, the Cooper Union Museum, New York; Mrs. James W. Marvin, Shelburne Museum, Shelburne, Vermont; Miss Edith A. Standen, The Metropolitan Museum of Art, New York; Miss Mildred B. Lanier, Colonial Williamsburg, Virginia; Mr. Peter Spang III, Mr. and Mrs. Henry N. Flynt, Heritage Foundation, Deerfield, Mass., my very deep appreciation of their complete understanding of the difficulty involved in selecting examples of work at so great a distance—their response to requests for detailed information has been of outstanding value.

My thanks too, to my students Philippa Haw, Sara Killick, Susan Condict, Margaret Fagg, and Margaret Silver, who have willingly given their help in experimental design; to Miss Lefa Fry for her patience in correcting the manuscript, to Mrs. Margareta F. Lyons for her work in designing the lay-out of the book, and to Miss Elinor Parker for the help she has given throughout its production.

6

Introduction

The term Florentine is used here to cover varieties of Florentine stitch and Hungarian point. These two stitches are distinct but the type of design on which they are used overlaps to such an extent that the two cannot be studied separately. Florentine stitch can be variously stepped, generally forming a zigzag line.

Flame or lightning patterns, developments of the zigzag, are formed with either Florentine or Hungarian point.

In certain elaborate floral designs Hungarian point is the dominant stitch forming a zigzag background as well as pattern on the motifs.

Groundings for use on canvas, mainly of 19th century origin, are based on Florentine stitch, Hungarian stitch and Hungarian point, and have an important part to play in present day canvas embroidery.

There is a tendency to think that certain stitches should always be used alone, Tent stitch (petit point) being an outstanding example of this belief, yet comparatively few pieces of historical embroidery have been worked entirely in one stitch. In Florentine embroidery not only are other stitches included, but very often part of the design is worked with stitches at right angles to the rest.

9

FLORENTINE EMBROIDERY

A most versatile type of embroidery, Florentine, if accepted in its widest sense, offers far greater scope for use today than if we restrict the connotation to the variety known as 'flame' which is indeed the least adaptable of all its forms. However, in its adaptation to present day use all Florentine methods call for considerable restraint in both choice of colour and scale of design.

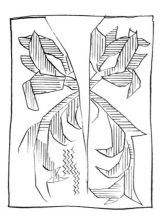

Fragment worked in floss silk on linen canvas
Probably Italian
Tulip-type flowers shaded pink to cream
Leaves shaded green—yellow-green
Background, an acid yellow worked in Byzantine stitch
  in a much coarser thread than the floral motif
Size 7½″ x 9″
Diagram to show direction of Florentine stitch 4.2 step

PART I | *History*

A chair seat embroidered in crewel wool in Florentine 4.2 step in a design which is a combination of flame and carnation patterns. The chair, now in Ashley House, Deerfield, was worked in 1776 by a 14 year old member of the Saltonstall family, and was one of a set made for their house in Haverhill, Mass. (ASHLEY HOUSE, DEERFIELD, MASS. PHOTO, TAYLOR & DULL)

INTRODUCTION

We do not know the origin of Florentine embroidery though it is easy to imagine that in some remote period in the evolution of needlework, a woman stitching in wool on coarse, loosely woven cloth found that she could cover a large area of fabric much more quickly if she worked vertical stitches between every other thread on the first row, and on the second row placed her stitches between them, than if she worked them side by side like satin stitch. This gave a reasonably smooth, closely covered surface, and any unevenness in colour resulting from vegetable dyes could be used to shade her interlocked background. Brick stitch, for such is the name given to her discovery, worked over an even number of threads, can be found in much early European embroidery, especially on the ecclesiastical work of mediaeval Germany, where it is used in elaborate designs, as well as in all-over patterns and borders. Sometimes the colour shades from dark to light in successive rows, working inwards to a bird or animal motif.

Possibly another needlewoman with an economical turn of mind, saw in the little 'up and down' pattern a chance to save wool, and produced a similar effect by stepping her stitches up one, down one, along the same row, with the next row interlocking with the last, to give an almost identical result; her discovery is now called Florentine stitch. The transition from this to a zigzag line is very slight, the chevron pattern having been known from time immemo-

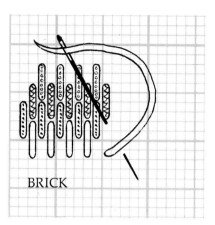

BRICK

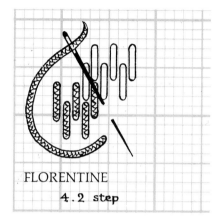

FLORENTINE

4.2 step

rial. The chevron pattern itself can often be found in diapered backgrounds in mediaeval embroidery, though produced by underside couching and not by any canvas stitch method. On an early 14th century German dalmatic the treatment of a chevron pattern with a double line of long stitches followed by a row of shorter stitches, is certainly a forerunner of Hungarian Point, in idea if not in technique. The same design can be found on a mid-14th century French almoner's pouch, again in couched gold thread. The basket pattern (See Part III, A3, page 81) on a mid-14th century Austrian altar curtain and on an Italian orphrey made c.1500, both worked in couched gold thread, is yet another example of continuity in design and thought.

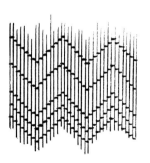

Chevron pattern
Underside couching in gold thread
Mediaeval European

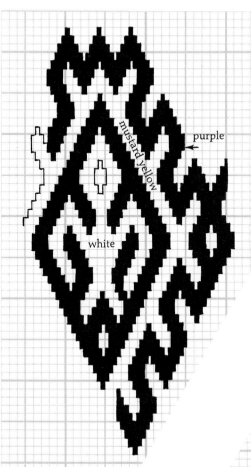

mustard yellow

purple

white

German, 14th century. Motif from a bag worked in brick stitch in coloured silks on linen. (VICTORIA & ALBERT MUSEUM) Compare the outer line with the Italian 17th century design, p. 23.

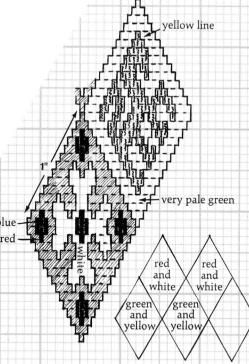

yellow line

very pale green

blue

red

1"

white

red and white	red and white
green and yellow	green and yellow

German, 14th century. A yellow lion rampant on a pale green ground, alternating with a white cross on a red ground; worked in brick stitch, 4.2 step, with fairly coarse silk on white linen. There is no shading. (VICTORIA & ALBERT MUSEUM)

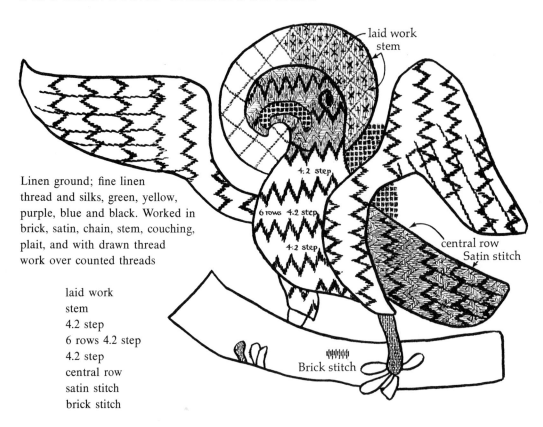

Linen ground; fine linen
thread and silks, green, yellow,
purple, blue and black. Worked in
brick, satin, chain, stem, couching,
plait, and with drawn thread
work over counted threads

laid work
stem
4.2 step
6 rows 4.2 step
4.2 step
central row
satin stitch
brick stitch

Eagle of Saint John from an altar curtain, Halberstadt Cathedral Museum. Lower Saxony
Late 13th-Early 14th century

Evidence that mediaeval craftsmen worked with a limited
colour range and shaded in self colour can be seen in English and
French illuminated manuscripts, in Italian Primitive paintings, in
tapestry and embroidery. Weaver and embroiderer discovered that
silk and wool reacted differently to the same dye, therefore the use of
both threads almost doubled the range; both craftsmen knew that
interlocked colours shaded gradually into one another when seen
from a distance. Florentine embroidery has evolved from such an
heritage and would appear to have existed long before it became
known by its present name which has acquired some air of mystery,
even romance.

16

There is danger in over-complicating the origin of a stitch which is essentially a development of a simple process; detailed study reveals the great variety of patterns obtainable from a regular use of vertical stitches arranged in different steps and blocks, and the emergence, probably sometime in the late 16th century, of two styles, one based on Florentine 4.2 step, and the other on Hungarian Point with several long and short steps.

It is interesting at this point to note Mrs. Christie's comment in *Samplers and Stitches* on Brick stitch shading. "The stitch is often found upon the English 17th century wool work hangings where so many examples of shading methods can be studied with advantage" She certainly considers it pre-eminently a shading stitch and goes on to state that it must be carried out with extreme regularity, all its stitches parallel with no radiation, as in long and short stitch.

Since Brick and much early Florentine stitch have a 4.2 step, (see pages 14 and 22) only examination of the back of the work will determine which stitch has been used. In some old examples Florentine, which can be very quickly worked in long diagonal lines, has pulled the canvas together to give the impression that the ground fabric was woven with two threads crossed by one thread rather like double mesh canvas, though in fact this was not the case.

The term Florentine embroidery embraces a group of stitches with a confusing assortment of names, perhaps acquired sometime during the late 16th or early 17th century when the real, creative advance was made in this type of canvas work. From this time onwards Hungarian Point, Point de Hongrie or Hungarian Ground play an increasing part in the design. Hungarian stitch is also used for shaded designs.

The name may have some connection with a legend, probably based on fact, that a Hungarian noblewoman, on her marriage to one of the Medici, brought the stitch to Italy on articles in her trousseau. The true origin of the most elaborate designs described as 'lightning' or 'flame', in Italian 'fiamme', is unknown. Another name, 'Bargello', seldom used nowadays, derives from the Bargello in Florence where seven chairs are still kept, relics from the days when the museum was a great patrician dwelling.

Terminology is still inconsistent. The name Hungarian Ground or Point should be restricted to those patterns with one or more rows of long stitches over 6 or 7 threads, followed by 2,3,4 or even 5 rows over 2 threads which produce a subsidiary zigzag pattern independent of colour. Other patterns should be grouped under Florentine stitch or be considered derivatives of that stitch, or they may be associated with Hungarian stitch.

The 17th century embroiderer's desire for more elaborate designs gave rise to further problems. Canvas lacked the polished regularity of today's factory product; quality and mesh might vary slightly from one piece of work to another. Colours, which even nowadays cannot always be guaranteed to match those of an earlier dye vat, were then matched with remarkable skill, but varied none the less. The value of contrast in both the colour and texture of wool and silk had long been recognised; to this was added the greater contrast between long and short stitches which came with the development of Hungarian point. Increasing elaboration of design brought a proportionate need for increased concentration on the part of the embroideress. Much work done in the past is irregular. Young Martha Edlin, on her tiny pincushion, had trouble with her counting, had to put in some extra stitches and skilfully covered up her mistakes. Many a needlewoman lost her way in her pattern's intricacies. In a large piece of work such mistakes are often hidden by the total richness and are found only by someone trying painstakingly to copy the design. The irregularity of much historical work adds greatly to its charm; this is not an excuse for bad technique, but should make us aware of the need for spontaneity and should stand as a warning against mere mechanical perfection.

Northern European familiarity with brick stitch and probably with Hungarian stitch and simple Florentine stitch facilitated the

HUNGARIAN STITCH

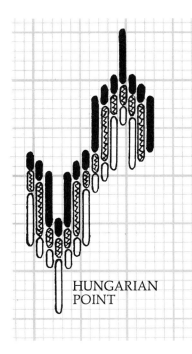

HUNGARIAN
POINT

Florentine stitch
yellowish ground
with dark blue-
green veins

Tent stitch

scale, 9 blocks across
turned leaf tip
Hungarian stitch

Hungarian
stitch

Part of a panel in the set of Hatton Garden
Hangings, English, late 17th century, in which
several leaves are worked in Hungarian stitch
(VICTORIA & ALBERT MUSEUM)

19

acceptance of Hungarian point and the Flame version of Florentine embroidery. Ideas spread more widely and rapidly than we sometimes realise and during their dispersal undergo changes befitting the countries where they take root, changes which may well improve upon the original. Craftsmen travel too and are not immune to the effects of artistic climate in the countries which they visit. Ideas may be tempered by economics, for every craftsman has to live by his trade. This may account for the divergence, in the 17th and 18th centuries, between the Italian and English interpretation of Florentine work.

Evidence that Florentine stitch and Hungarian point were in use on upholstery as early as the 17th century is slender, but Hungarian point containing long stitches is not as enduring as some other methods and it would be reasonable to suppose that sets of chairs worked at that time have since needed to be re-upholstered. When this was done the needlewoman may sometimes have copied the original design and, to the best of her ability, the colour.

There are four clearly defined styles:

1. Designs worked in Florentine stitch, 4.2 step
2. Floral designs worked in Hungarian point with some other stitches
3. Flame patterns worked in Florentine, generally in 4.2 step
4. Flame patterns worked in Hungarian point

All these methods were in use at the same time in England and Europe, and by the 18th century had spread to North America where the fashion was enthusiastically accepted and the range of articles to be decorated widened to include purses, pocketbooks, bench covers and window drapes, as well as the pockets, shoes, toilet and lace boxes, hand-screens and day-beds made in England. Some such small objects must also have been made in 17th and 18th century Italy, for it is hard to believe that Florentine embroidery was restricted there to bed and table covers, curtains, upholstery and ecclesiastical work. Undoubtedly the best work in all four styles was produced during the late 17th and the 18th centuries. The 19th century has little of interest to offer apart from a variety of geometric patterns on samplers where some very attractive groundings were created, occasionally in charming colour; on the whole Victorian wool embroidery suffered from ill-considered tone values, not helped by some very harsh colours, the result of inexperience on the part of wool dyers in the use of newly discovered aniline dyes.

Until recently the 20th century embroiderer on canvas has made only a limited contribution to the development of the craft. However, in the years following World War II embroidery has re-emerged as a creative art, demonstrating as in the case of certain other crafts, notably stained glass and fabric design, the new awareness of colour and texture which has grown throughout the artistic world.

1. DESIGNS WORKED IN FLORENTINE STITCH 4.2 STEP; designs which are not floral, with Florentine stitch predominant; designs strongly influenced by the flame pattern which may form part of the design

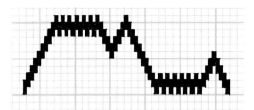

Italian, 17th century. Florentine fragment worked in floss silk on coarse canvas. Flame design in 4.2 step. Diagonal lines are worked normally; horizontal lines are worked to and fro. As so often found, too many colours are used for an harmonious result. The design is a forerunner of the flame pattern.
(VICTORIA & ALBERT MUSEUM)

Colour arrangement:

black
3 rows shaded gold
yellow
cream
pale cream
2 rows pale blue
sky blue
blackish brown
2 rows fawn-gold
3 rows deep cream
yellow
yellow green
mid green
deep green
black
repeat

Italian, 17th century. Fragment of a border pattern worked in Florentine stitch in coloured silk on fine canvas. A very simple design closely akin to patterns in brick stitch found on mediaeval German embroidery. (VICTORIA & ALBERT MUSEUM)

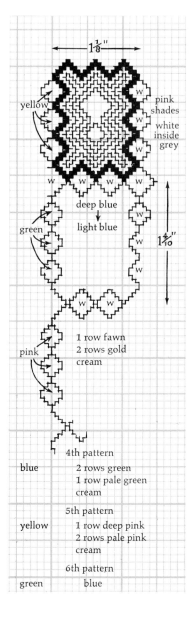

yellow

pink shades
white inside grey

deep blue
light blue

green

1$\frac{1}{8}$″

1$\frac{4}{10}$″

pink

1 row fawn
2 rows gold
cream

blue

4th pattern
2 rows green
1 row pale green
cream

yellow

5th pattern
1 row deep pink
2 rows pale pink
cream

6th pattern

green

blue

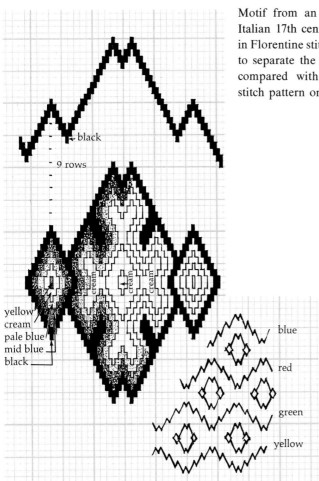

Motif from an extremely irregular, much joined, Italian 17th century cover, worked in silk on linen, in Florentine stitch, 4.2 step, with a shaded flame line to separate the motifs. The inner shape should be compared with the German 14th century brick stitch pattern on p. 15.

An Italian 17th century design in Florentine stitch, 4.2 step, worked in floss silk on canvas. The pattern, outlined in black, interlocks vertically. Fairly large areas of background filled in with gold silk serve to alleviate the sickly pinks and greens used in alternate repeats. Compare with the fragment in the Victoria & Albert Museum on page 24.

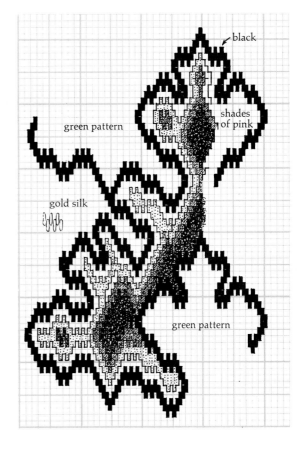

FLORENTINE EMBROIDERY

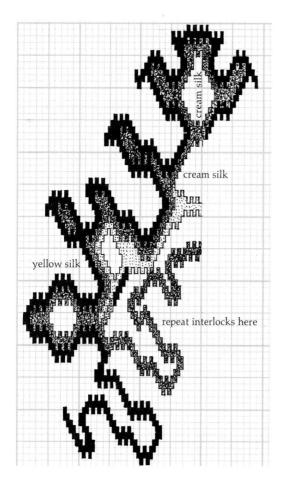

cream silk

cream silk

yellow silk

repeat interlocks here

An Italian 17th century fragment, possibly of a curtain; a complicated interlocking vertical repeat worked in wool in Florentine stitch, 4.2 step, against a silk background of Hungarian point. The colour juxtaposition, seen unfaded on the back, is unpleasantly gaudy and arranged very inconsistently. Two rows, shades of dark turquoise, form a strong outline; other colours used include various pinks, crimson and salmon, bright hard green and yellow-green, two shades of ultramarine blue, ginger-brown and gold. Compare with page 23. (VICTORIA & ALBERT MUSEUM)

An Italian 17th or 18th century altar frontal, 62″ x 41″ combines in its design two entirely different styles. The central field, apart from an oval medallion edged with flowers to match the border and containing the symbolic vine, is covered with a formal carnation and rose pattern worked in cross stitch. The three borders show very strongly the influence of Greek Island embroidery with stylised flower vases supported by confronted stags, worked in satin and stem stitch. The colours in field and border include blue, pink, brown, green and white. The whole background is in yellow silk Florentine stitch, 4.2 step. (THE METROPOLITAN MUSEUM OF ART, ANONYMOUS GIFT, 1955)

24

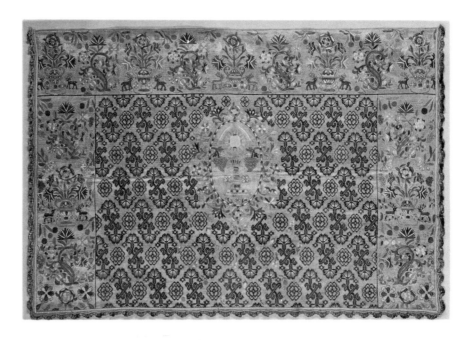

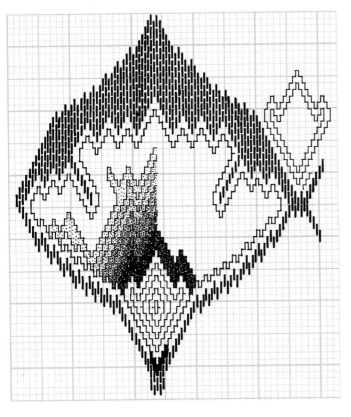

Cartoon of Alexander fragment
carnation pattern, blue flower

A wallet, 8¼″ long x 9″ wide (open) 4½″ wide (closed), embroidered in crewel wool on
canvas, with a carnation design in Florentine 4.2 step. The owner's name and date, William
Kingsley 1773, is worked in cross stitch along the fold; probably American, now in the
Helen Geier Flynt Fabric Hall, Deerfield, Mass.

Colours used on William Kingsley wallet (right)

Wools

green	dark purple
lime green	brownish red
lemon yellow	dark pink
black	light pink
white	light lavender
reddish brown	dark purple
orange	bright red
dark yellow	pink
lemon yellow	dark blue
dark green	light blue
light lavender	

Binding
dark green

Lining
heliotrope

Name worked in green

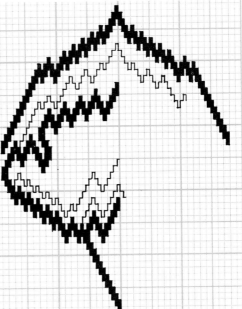

bottle green ↗ ↘ naturalistic curve

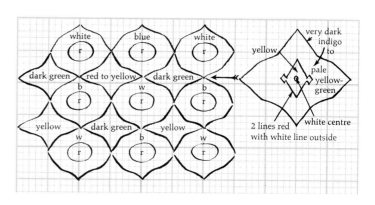

white · · · blue · · · white · · · yellow · · · very dark indigo to
r · · · r · · · r · · · pale yellow-green
dark green · red to yellow · dark green
b · · · w · · · b
r · · · r · · · r
yellow · · · dark green · · · yellow · · · 2 lines red · white centre
w · · · b · · · w · with white line outside
r · · · r · · · r

English Chair seat, c.1750–75, worked in wool and silk on canvas in Florentine stitch, 4.2 step. The motif, a stylised yet easily recognisable carnation, a flower which continued in popularity from the Elizabethan period when it had so often been enclosed within a scroll, here is surrounded by a flame stitch line reversed to form an ogival pattern. The colours are crude. All the carnations are in shades of a plum red, against alternately a white ground and an unshaded blue ground. Intervening flame shapes are alternately dark green to indigo, and yellow through cream to orange brown. (VICTORIA & ALBERT MUSEUM, CROWN COPYRIGHT)

26

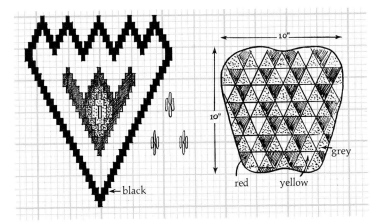

English 18th century hand screen, also initialled and dated 1718. Each red triangle has a shaded green centre; each yellow triangle has old gold, fawn and cream, and all the grey triangles have three small cream spots. (VICTORIA & ALBERT MUSEUM)

English 18th century hand screen panel, silk on linen canvas. Initialled and dated 1718. Florentine stitch, 4.2 step. Colour, cream and pale blue alternating with apricot and cream, separated by a pale green shaded flame line. An occasional bright pink line is shown in the sketch. (VICTORIA & ALBERT MUSEUM)

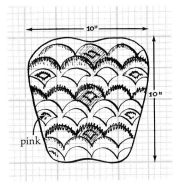

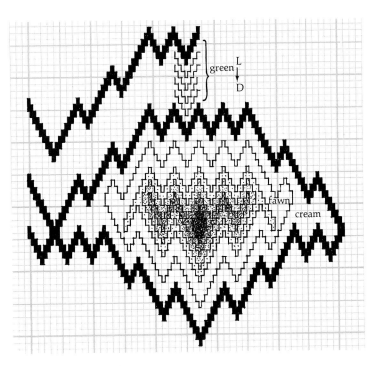

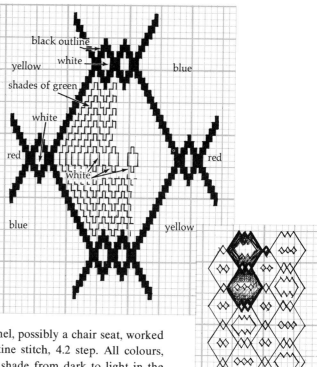

black outline
yellow white blue
shades of green
white
red red
white
blue yellow

English late 18th century panel, possibly a chair seat, worked in silk on canvas in Florentine stitch, 4.2 step. All colours, red, green, blue and yellow shade from dark to light in the centre; they are harsh and only partly helped by the black outline. (VICTORIA & ALBERT MUSEUM)

The ecclesiastical use of Florentine stitch was not confined to the Christian church. Two Ark curtains, both Italian, one in the Victoria & Albert Museum and the other dated 1676, on loan to the Jewish Museum, Woburn Place, London, are recognisably 17th century design. The present subdued colour is only partially due to fading. Both are worked in coloured silks on linen canvas, in either Florentine or brick stitch 4.2 step, one arranged vertically and the other horizontally. Hebrew script, in slightly raised satin stitch, in silver thread, stands out in clear contrast. A very little shading is used on conventionalised acanthus-type leaves, on clouds above the Tablets of the Law and in the background of soil behind plants in a garden beneath the Tablets. Though interesting neither curtain is beautiful.

28

2. FLORAL DESIGNS worked mainly in either Florentine stitch or Hungarian point

The seventeenth century Italian floral style which as far as we know developed at the same time as the flame pattern, is a true product of the Renaissance, flamboyantly designed with scrolling acanthus foliage and naturalistic birds, worked in Hungarian point with some additional stitches, often against a gold silk background.

Many fragments have found their way into museums and private collections. Our pleasure in a colour scheme now mellow and subtle is somewhat tempered when the unfaded reverse side is examined and the discovery made that while deep blues and greens remain largely unaltered, various bright salmon pinks once took the place of today's soft mushroom, and mauves supplanted greyish blue. Yellow silk, which absorbed its dye with aggressive intensity, suffers comparatively little, though where it has toned down the effect is far richer than its embroiderer could have conceived.

A long panel, 9′ x 2′ (V. & A.), illustrated on p. 34 appears restrained in contrast to the exuberance of some other examples in which cabbage-like flowers and leaves in 4.2 step have some petals worked at right angles, while, in the same piece of work, peacocks and parrots in 2.1 step give the impression of being embroidered in tent stitch; all these motifs are in natural colours against a strong yellow silk ground of mosaic stitch.

Another piece of work in the Victoria and Albert Museum, a very large cover, may have been intended for either a bed or a table. The plain centre filled with quickly worked diagonal rows of Florentine stitch allows the main interest to be concentrated in the border where acanthus leaves scroll between Turk's cap lilies, carnations, rose-buds, stylised flowers and easily recognisable birds, dove, thrush, jay and goldfinch, in natural colours. Couched metal thread outlines all the motifs.

An Italian late 17th or early 18th century cloth, 102″ square, now at Parham, has an applied 12″ wide border of scrolling acanthus-style leaves and heavy flowers, embroidered in silk in shades of red, green, yellow, stone, blue and pale mauve, in Florentine stitch over six threads stepping back inconsistently two or three; the stitch is used in both directions; a few French knots can be found among the flowers. The background is entirely in cream silk, in a diamond pattern, a version of Hungarian *stitch*. These three pieces of work have much in common.

While Italian embroiderers were content to rely on foliage strongly influenced by the classical Roman style, English embroiderers continued to find ideas in their own gardens, though at this time they found even more inspiration in Dutch flower paintings, an influence to be seen in a chocolate brown armchair made about 1675, lavishly decorated with rather heavy peonies, carnations and other flowers, and stylised foliage, worked in long and short, tent, split and satin stitch, in silk and wool on canvas, with a background of Hungarian point which defies analysis, for the stitches are of all lengths and not entirely in the same direction. Whether this very beautiful piece of embroidery, so obviously in its creation a labour of love, was worked by an elderly woman with failing sight and stiffening fingers, or simply by someone who was not a good technician, we shall never know. Irregularity in the basic fabric may have created difficulties, and stray stitches which had to be fitted in around complicated shapes inevitably threw out the counting, one adjustment led to another until it would seem the embroiderer gave up the unequal struggle to count at all. The plants, now subdued in colour to soft blues, greens and creamy yellows, spread out freely against the dark ground to give a design of great charm and richness. No matter what difficulties were encountered in its making, this chair would still today be a joy to possess.

The distribution of such floral upholstery on chairs and set-tees, in which Hungarian point predominates, must have been fairly widespread. Of a set of high-backed chairs at Drayton House,* six have been re-covered during this century, copying the original design, six retain their 17th century upholstery. All have a very dark brown wool background with a large floral spray on the seat and a flower-filled urn on the back, chiefly in reds and blues with a little cream. Long and short, and tent stitch are used for detail in the flowers. Hungarian point background stitchery is irregular, one chair has zigzag rows of one long stitch followed by two rows of short stitches, two chairs are entirely in long stitches over six threads in chevron pattern, and three chairs have one long stitch row followed by one short. Such lack of uniformity is of little consequence when the great size of the room in which they stand is taken into account for two chairs would rarely, if ever, be seen together.

In this period of grandiose architectural schemes it is hardly surprising that the scale of some furniture should follow suit; yet even when State beds grew upwards several feet, the increased area did not deter embroiderers.

Bed hanging fragments of considerable importance can be seen at Boughton House, Kettering, where a settee, two chairs and two stools have in recent years been re-covered with material origi-nally embroidered for a State bed (though probably not, as locally believed, in preparation for a visit to the house by William and Mary in 1694, for that bed is now, complete with hangings, in the V. & A.). The fabric has been cut very skillfully to fit the furniture without too much damage or wastage, even so it is extremely difficult to visualise the arrangement of the panels in their original place, for valances and narrow borders have been separated in the scheme of re-creation. However, it is known that the centre panel of the bed measured 9' high by 8' wide and that there were two panels at either corner at the foot. Hungarian point varying one long two short, one long one

* Lowick, Kettering, Northamptonshire

31

short, is worked in both directions on the canvas. The light tone of the ivory cream silk ground acts as a foil for the wool floral sprays worked chiefly in red, blue and brown, with some blue-grey, green, yellow and grey. The regal effect of this colour scheme, and a design still closely associated with Italian detail must now be left to the imagination. (See Appendix)

Fortunately the hangings on the State Bed at Drayton House are perfectly preserved. These were made between 1660 and 1680 to the order of the 2nd Earl of Peterborough, and include an embroidered cornice, top and mattress valances, narrow curtains and wider cantonnières (corner curtains), all worked on canvas and still retaining the original green velvet lining. No tradition has been handed down as to their origin, nor has there been found any record of purchase or the name of the worker. Both omissions are curious, since if purchased the hangings would have been very costly, and if locally produced a record of fees paid should exist. Perhaps one day these interesting facts may come to light. Though technically similar to the work at Boughton there are differences in design; the acanthus foliage is far removed from the Renaissance treatment of the plant, and classical urns used at intervals in the cantonnières are all that remain of Italian influence now unmistakably supplanted by that of Dutch flower painting . . . peonies, large carnations and smaller pinks; bizarre, feathered and flamed tulips; the crown imperial lily; daffodils, hyacinths and fritillaries; hollyhocks, campanulas, roses, and many other flowers all closely packed together, could have been transferred directly from painter's to embroiderer's canvas. In this unique adoption of flower painting as the model for bed-curtains, the adaptation to design is in scale with the bed; the work appears professional in drawing and stitchery. The dark brown wool ground, at times verging on black, is worked entirely in Hungarian point, one long, one short stitch. The few urns are in tent stitch, while on the flowers, tent, long and short and most haphazardly worked Hungarian point are chosen for their imitative value . . . spotted fritillaries in tent stitch, peonies

32

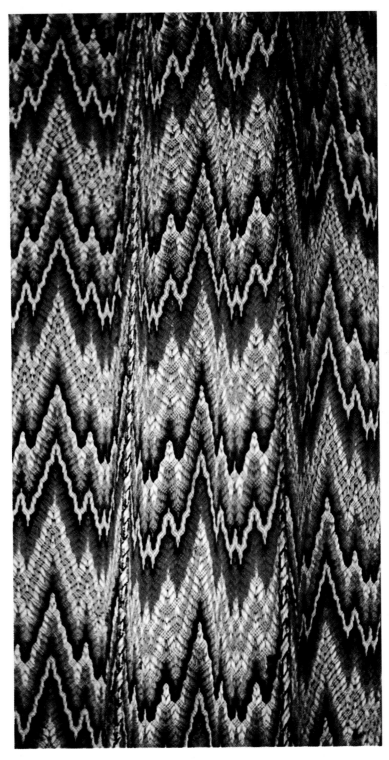

I. Detail of a bed curtain at Parham Park, Sussex

in Hungarian point in both directions and the use of long and short shading in the tulips would come near to needle painting were the colours more naturalistic. This may have been the embroiderer's aim; fortunately it was not the result. Whether or not this great piece of embroidery was done in England or abroad, the dye colours include familiar shades of indigo blues and a little bluish-green, various reds, cream and a little golden brown shading to yellow. Widely scattered detail in cream silk sparkles against the dark ground. These curtains

Drayton House—state bed

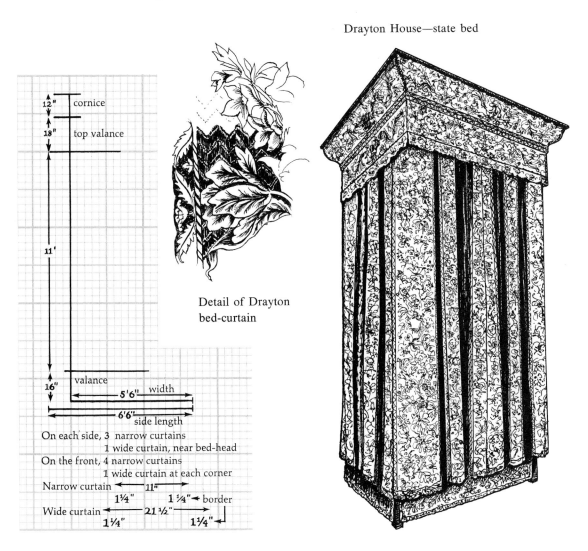

12" cornice

18" top valance

11'

Detail of Drayton
bed-curtain

16" valance

5'6" width

6'6" side length

On each side, 3 narrow curtains
1 wide curtain, near bed-head
On the front, 4 narrow curtains
1 wide curtain at each corner
Narrow curtain ← 11" →
1¼" 1¼" ← border
Wide curtain ← 21½" →
1¼" 1¼"

are lined with deep olive green velvet, panels of which hang between those which are embroidered, enhancing the richness. Like the Parham bed-hangings (p. 55) these represent the apogee of their particular style.

Panel of 17th century Italian embroidery, 4' x 11" including surrounding 1" border.

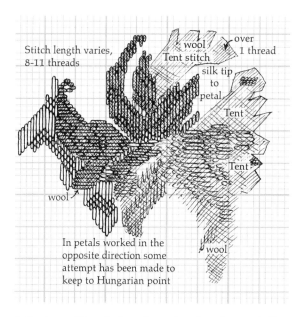

A freely scrolling design of acanthus type leaves, tulips, roses and various conventionalised flowers worked in Hungarian point in two directions, some untidy long and short stitch, tent stitch and French knots, in colours now pleasantly softened from pink to mushroom, and mauve to greyish blue and greyish fawn, with some deep blues and greens retaining their original hue; all against a gold floss silk background of Hungarian point. (VICTORIA & ALBERT MUSEUM, CROWN COPYRIGHT)

34

3. FLAME PATTERNS generally in Florentine stitch 4.2 step

The Flame or Lightning pattern can be worked either in Florentine 4.2 step or in Hungarian point. Complete examples of either method are extremely difficult to trace. In Italy the set of seven chairs in the Bargello may well be the best extant specimens in that country. Other examples must be scattered throughout Europe, the British Isles and America in museums and private collections, but as no definitive list of their whereabouts has ever been compiled, they are generally to be found quite by chance.

Englishwomen were familiar with the flame line for many years before it eventually came into fashion and it would be interesting to discover why it took such an unconscionably long time to become established, long enough indeed for the idea to die out entirely rather than to burst suddenly into life about a hundred years after its introduction.

An unusual example of the flame pattern can be seen at Parham Park,* where, in the West Room, two walls are hung with curtains each 5'6" x 20'. The large zigzag pattern repeats in shades of blue, brown and fawn; yellow through pinkish beige to rust red; yellowish tones through orange and fawn to blue; the whole dominated by the recurrent strong blue lines. The curtains came from Quenby Hall in Leicestershire, and are late 16th century, probably before 1590, and are known to be incomplete, part having been cut and made into chair seats which are unlikely to have survived, for the long rather loose stitches would not submit to hard wear. The stitch looks remarkably like knitting or even long chain stitch and is a very early experiment in the flame pattern, but the unusual technique precludes it from being classified as Hungarian point. These curtains are probably unique and may represent the earliest known attempt at a flame design.

There may be some truth in the legend that during a time of hardship, Elizabeth of Hungary devised this economically worked stitch for the peasants to use on their embroideries, scarcely any wool being wasted on the back. The design eventually reached Italy where, combined with Hungarian point, the accepted flame pattern seems to have originated. The version which appears on English early 17th century samplers and again in the 18th century samplers worked in England, Germany, Mexico and Spain, has the flame line worked in Florentine stitch, usually 4.2, sometimes 6.1 step.

The Carew-Pole Collection* contains several provocative fragments, scarcely to be called samplers, yet apparently test pieces, some

* Private collection

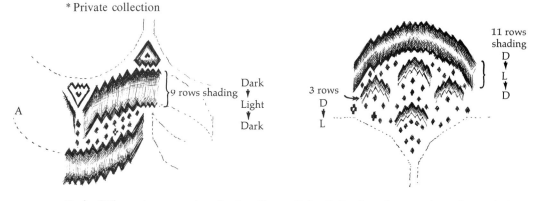

Early 17th century samplers in the Carew Pole Collection show various flame designs worked in Florentine stitch, 4.2 step.—an unfinished panel in coloured wool on linen canvas, 22½″ x 11″, two unfinished panels in coloured silk on linen canvas, 22½″ x 23½″ and 22½″ x 24″, two fragments in coloured silk on linen canvas, 13½″ x 3¾″ and 17½″ x 13½″. (See London Walpole Society, Vol. 221.)

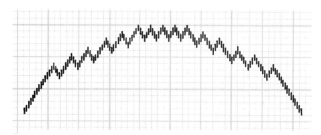

According to A. J. B. Wace these fragments could be 18th century but for the 22½″ canvas which has a blue thread in the selvedge, a peculiarity of the late 16th and early 17th century. The width 22½″ is also found about 1600. There seems a marked continuity in thought between these samplers, the W. J. Holt chair and the carnation chair seats.

worked in wool, others in silk on linen canvas 22½″ wide, which, according to A. J. B. Wace, can be dated c.1600 by a blue thread running through the selvedge, though apart from this peculiarity the work might be late 17th or early 18th century. If we compare these fragments with the Parham embroideries there is less reason to doubt their early date. The upholstery of the handsome chair once owned by W. J. Holt Esq, below, appears to be a development of the Carew-Pole designs and this may have been started earlier than believed and mounted soon after the completion of the framework itself.

Undoubtedly some forms of Florentine stitch can be worked more quickly than others and it may be that this knowledge influenced, in the 17th century, the choice of design and stitch for the fabric now covering a large set of furniture at Boughton House, Kettering. So often single pieces of work are seen in isolation and we

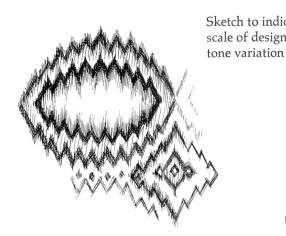

Sketch to indicate scale of design and tone variation

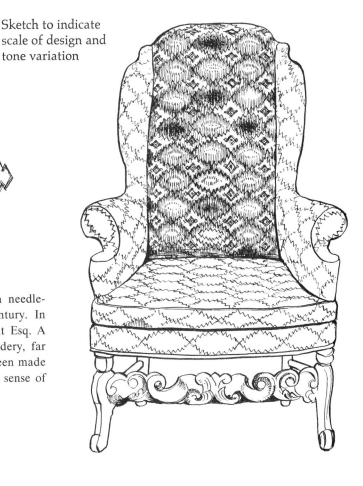

High-backed arm chair c.1680 with needle-work probably very early 18th century. In 1928 in the collection of W. J. Holt Esq. A rich and beautiful piece of embroidery, far more varied in tone than if it had been made today, and illustrates well the inate sense of design which knew not rigidity.

fail to grasp the true significance of their place in a colour scheme which in fact may cover a very large total area. All this upholstery, embroidered entirely in silk, in Florentine stitch, 6.1 step, in a bold flame pattern with a large repeat (above) is of a much lighter tone than believed usual at the time. The general colour scheme is green,

Below. Design from an Italian 17th century fragment worked in floss silk on canvas. 4.2 step. (VICTORIA & ALBERT MUSEUM)

Florentine 6.2 step

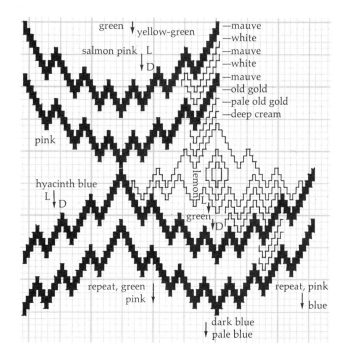

Sketch to indicate size of repeat
Chair, Boughton House

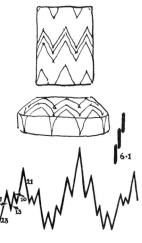

Colour arrangement:
  Pale green

  ↓ 7 shades

  Very dark blue-green
  Single black line
  Burnt sienna brown
    sometimes with 1 line
    red among
    darkest browns
  ↓ 6 shades

  cream
  repeat very pale green

brown and cream, with variation in shades and the order of their use. Some variation occurs too in the number of stitches building up each point in the flame design which is crossed by an inconspicuous subsidiary zigzag pattern. The very large size of the repeat and the large quantity of work might well have been irritating to live with were it not for the colour scheme. Particularly when new, the sheen on the silk thread contributed its own brightness to the soft lighter tones which dominate, and the whole effect must have appeared fresh and gay in the extremely lofty room where the furniture was placed. However, it cannot be said that large repeats were kept for large rooms. The Deerfield bed curtains (p. 41) and rug (p. 40), Shelburne window draperies (p. 42) and a day-bed and chair at Colonial Williamsburg are sufficient to contradict this assumption.

An Italian 18th century panel, 32″ x 24½″ embroidered on canvas in Florentine stitch in coloured silks, red, pink, lavender, blues, greens, grey cream, yellow, brown and white. There is little unity between the design of the central field and the floral scroll border worked in split stitch and French knots. (THE METROPOLITAN MUSEUM OF ART, GIFT OF MRS. SAMUEL STIEFEL)

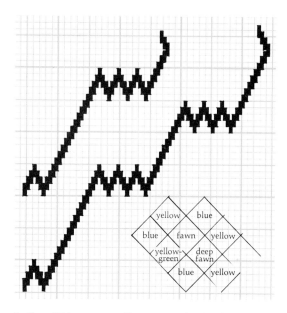

Italian 17th century. Fragment of a border pattern worked in Florentine stitch in coloured silk on fine canvas. A very simple design closely akin to patterns in brick stitch found on mediaeval German embroidery (VICTORIA AND ALBERT MUSEUM)

English wing chair, probably late 17th-early 18th century. Now in Dwight-Barnard House, Deerfield, Mass. Stitch count in one repeat, below.

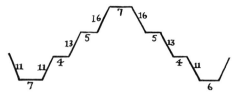

Colours used in one end repeat on the carpet at Deerfield. There are 4 repeats in the 34″ width, with minor variations in each, the two end repeats have more pink and the two in the centre have more purple. (DWIGHT-BARNARD HOUSE)

Light brown
fawn
greenish yellow
dark green
fawn
pinkish red
pinkish red, deeper
greenish yellow
pinkish red, deep
pinkish red
fawn
dark green
pale green
greenish yellow
fawn
purple
very dark brown
light brown
paler brown
pinkish red, deep
pinkish red
fawn
very dark brown
dark blue
light blue
paler blue
fawn

Bed curtains and top and mattress valances, worked about 1750, now hanging on a bed in Sheldon-Hawks House, Deerfield, are probably European. In the hangings themselves colour shades through brown to cream, dark blue to grey, and dark green to very light green, while in the pelmet more delicate shades of almost the same colours have been used, light brown and red to fawn, dark green to fawn, dark blue to fawn. The curtains are 6′5″ long and 7′3″ wide. The shallow rococo line of the pelmet varies from 10¼″–12½″ deep. The number of stitches in each point in the design varies somewhat from one repeat to another. The effect of this design worked in Florentine stitch, 6.1 step, makes an interesting comparison with the Parham bed which, also in flame pattern, is worked in Hungarian point. (p. 55)

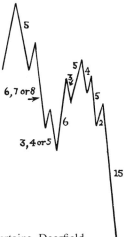

Stitch count, bed curtains, Deerfield

FLORENTINE EMBROIDERY

The Deerfield carpet, 64″ x 34″, worked about 1730, is thought to be European. The blue floral border, tufted by hand, could be of a different date and raises the question as to whether the carpet was originally part of a wall hanging, later adapted to its present use by the addition of the border.

Few early small objects survive in England but a flame pattern pincushion worked by Martha Edlin, born in 1660, shows what was then expected of a little girl. Numerous purses and wallets can be found in America indicating that the flame pattern must have been extremely popular throughout the 18th century.

Curtains and chair, Shelburne Museum. Florentine stitch, 6.2 step. (SHELBURNE MUSEUM, INC.)

Irregularities in the stitch count on the Italian bedspread worked about 1700, in no way detract from its handsome design. The sharp points are in 6.2 step and it is the blunt end that an extra stitch appears to have been wedged in. The shallow curves are worked by the 'to and fro' method which gives a closely interlocking surface. (See Part II, working method.)

The flame pattern is worked in two and three ply woollen yarns in shades of beige, white, blue and dark yellow-green shaded to mustard-gold and accented with black. A heavy natural linen fringe is decorated with tufts of mustard-gold wool.

A small bag, 7½″ x 6½″, in Dwight-Barnard House, Deerfield, also combines the blunt and pointed flame pattern. The final shape of the bag resulted from the design. It is worked in five shades of rose and five shades of brown, in each case to a very pale shade. Ball tassels decorate the corners. Diagram to show shape of flame line used in the design, and position of handle and ball tassels.

A long fragment now mounted as a runner, in the Wells-Thorn House Keeping Room, Deerfield, is also akin to these, and has festoons in wide shaded bands of gold, red, white, blue and pink. Since there are several matching pieces in the collection, these may all originally have been curtains.

43

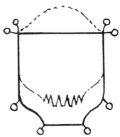

Numerous purses, wallets and pocket books were embroidered in Florentine stitch, 4.2 step, with variations of the zigzag line. One, rather more ambitious, to be seen at Colonial Williamsburg, uses a line similar to that on Martha Edlin's sampler p. 45, reversed to form compartments which are filled with different shades of wool. These wallets, apt to suffer from hard wear, must have been convenient small gifts, made all the more welcome by their usefulness.

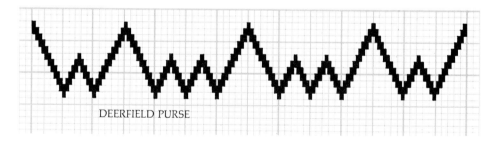

DEERFIELD PURSE

The American folding purse or wallet from Allen House, Deerfield, Mass., is worked on canvas in fine crewel wool in shades of blue, yellow, green, red and brown. It is lined with vermilion cambric and bound with olive green ribbon.

44

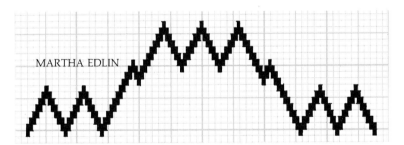

Martha Edlin, born in 1660, finished all her samplers by the time she was eleven. On her little pincushion, one of the many small articles made for her needlework box, the colours shade from very pale pink to red, white, indigo and are then repeated. She used silk on fine canvas, made many mistakes but hid them cleverly.

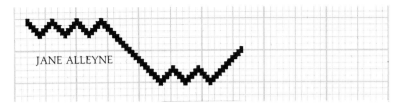

Jane Rollstone Alleyne, in the late 17th or early 18th century, worked on her fine linen sampler bands of pattern in rococo, rice, cross, satin and chain stitch, and buttonhole and needlepoint fillings. She used Florentine stitch, over 4 back 2, as a background to a stylised floral motif, the colours shading in a repeat through yellow-green, dark green, yellow-green, 3 rows natural, 3 pink, 3 yellow, 3 blue, 3 pink, each shading light, dark, light.

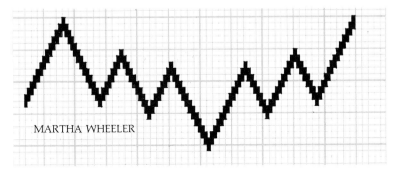

Twelve year old Martha Wheeler, in 1710, also working over 4 back 2, on similar material, but less competently, shaded through dark brown, 4 yellows, light to dark, fawn, brown; after two repeats she changed to two of pink and red, not a pretty colour scheme.

Left and above. Flame stitch patterns from English samplers and a purse at Deerfield, Mass.

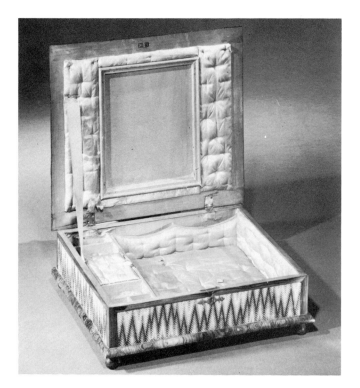

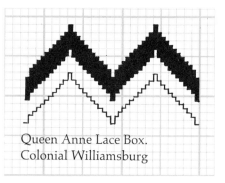

Queen Anne Lace Box.
Colonial Williamsburg

English Queen Anne Lace Box, embroidered with floss silk in shades of light green, beige and light brown, with a walnut veneer edging, and a padded interior, lined with rose pink China silk.

46

Above. A shoe, c.1720–40, on a clog, c.1730. Worked in Florentine stitch, 4.2 step, in silk on fine canvas. The colour, chiefly blue, green and cream, has no regular repeat. (VICTORIA & ALBERT MUSEUM)

Above left. A pocket, dated 1778, about 14″ deep, embroidered with worsteds, in Florentine stitch, the zigzags increasing from 6 at the top to 12 at the bottom. (VICTORIA & ALBERT MUSEUM)

English Queen Anne walnut veneered toilet box embroidered with very fine silk and wool in shades of rose, blue, green, gold, tan and light brown. The top of the box is worked in a flame pattern similar in step to a fragment in the Victoria and Albert Museum (Cartoon p. 22), except that here it is used in a continuous line and not turned round to form a compartment, (see also the seat pad design Part V, p. 128). The front and sides of the box have a design of flowering trees and flowers worked in rococo stitch. The box is 10″ x 12″, padded inside and lined with rose China silk. It is said to have come from the Foulke family whose ancestors came to America with William Penn in 1682.

47

4. FLAME PATTERNS
worked in Hungarian point

The ingenuity and patience needed to perfect a flame line worked in Hungarian point can be fully appreciated only when attempting to make a cartoon of one of the designs. Many slight variations in the shape of the line can be found on historical examples. The creation of new patterns is harder than might be expected; the clue to success lies in the accuracy of the thread count in a vertical line; once a pattern has been assigned to a certain type, for example, E2 (see Part III), then throughout a vertical line will be found two long stitches followed by two short. This fact is of utmost help in continuing any of the cartoons which are given. There can be no canvas embroidery in which it is easier to become hopelessly lost.

Italian embroiderers in particular exploited Hungarian point flame patterns, using them on vestments and altar frontals, bed hangings and wall curtains. Not content with an elaborate design for the main field of the work, they created extraordinary twisted border patterns of shaded bells and tassels with the edge sometimes cut out to follow their shape. Bells worked to a straight edge can be seen on the altar frontal p. 50 and on a shaped edge on the Parham bed valance p. 55. The large scale of most Hungarian point flame patterns allowed for a wide range of colour, usually delicately shaded, but with sudden strong tone contrasts which completely disguised the actual repeat.

Apart from the work at Parham the style does not seem to be well represented in England where floral designs were preferred. It may have found greater favour in 18th century America. A day-bed at Colonial Williamsburg is similar to some English chairs also in the same collection, but many examples which appear to be Hungarian point prove on closer inspection to be worked in Florentine stitch 6.1 step.

48

RIGHT: English 17th century chair back, Alexander fragment. *Courtesy of the Embroiderers' Guild*

BELOW: Detail showing both sides of the matching chair seat (white line divides front and back). *Author's collection.*

Fragments are from a set of late 17th century chairs worked in a carnation design in Florentine stitch, 4.2 step, in silk and wool, the latter mostly decayed, on unevenly woven canvas. [The colours include shades of indigo blue, a clear yellow, a dull yellow probably on an iron mordant, an unshaded deep rich madder red for the background, and a black outline. The blue flowers probably had white silk petals and the others shades of pale yellow.] A similar chair seat in the Victoria and Albert Museum is dated early 18th century. Both designs are strongly associated with the flame pattern but because they contain the carnation motifs are placed in the first group in this historical survey.

Italian 17th century chair in the Bargello, Florence, embroidered in Hungarian point. Though now faded, the general colour effect must have been in various shades of green and yellow.
Sketch to show size of repeat.

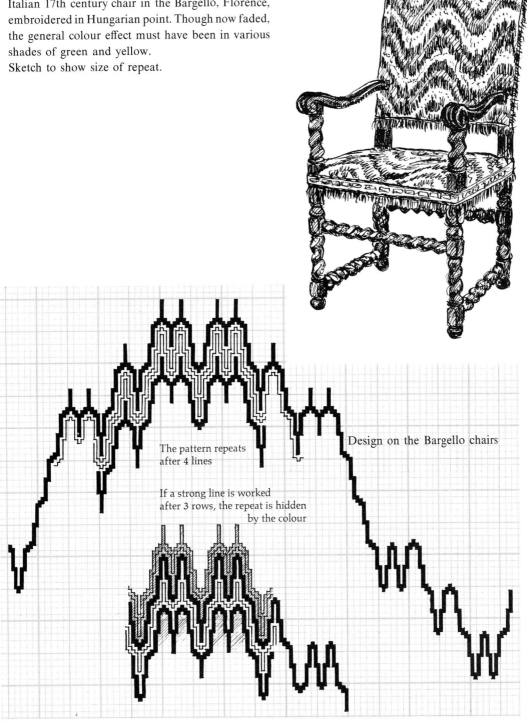

The pattern repeats
after 4 lines

Design on the Bargello chairs

If a strong line is worked
after 3 rows, the repeat is hidden
by the colour

Italian 17th century altar frontal

Colours used
      fairly strong golden yellow shading to greenish brown wool
      dark brown
   heavy silk—3 rows cream
      dark brown
      soft greys shading to soft pinks, deepening to
      brown
   silk—3 rows cream
      brown
      deep indigo blue-green
      deep green shading through mid green to soft yellowing green
      pale grey
      brown
   silk—3 rows cream
      brown
      pale grey shading to pink

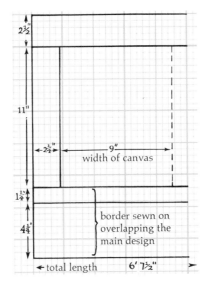

border sewn on overlapping the main design

width of canvas

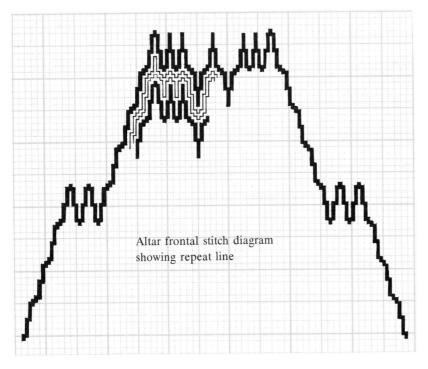

Altar frontal stitch diagram
showing repeat line

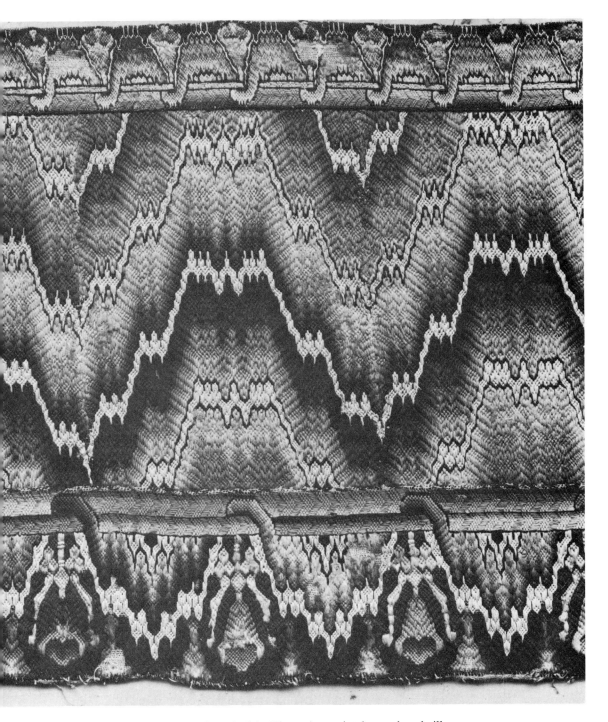

Italian 17th century altar frontal worked in Hungarian point in wool and silk on canvas.
(VICTORIA & ALBERT MUSEUM, CROWN COPYRIGHT)

51

If the altar frontal is compared with the Parham Park bed hangings certain similarities are
at once apparent, in the flame stitch line, subdued colour, the curious twisted effect in the
border, and in the narrow canvas on which both are worked. Though rich in general effect,
the altar frontal is in every way technically inferior to the hangings. This photograph shows
very clearly the subsidiary pattern formed by Hungarian point.

A chasuble, probably Italian, late 17th–early 18th century, worked in silk on linen in flame patterns, in Hungarian point and Florentine stitch. The vestment is trimmed, front, back and round the neck, with silver braid; the edges are finished with narrow gold lace; it is lined with cream linen. The back is made of three separate panels, the joins covered with silver braid. In the centre the colours blue, rose and cream predominate.

There are sections at shoulder-level, right and left, of Florentine stitch, 4.2 step, in lighter colours; again, lower right and left, are similar sections. These, particularly the section at the right, are worn enough to show the basic linen.

Shading in the centre panel runs:

> Light blue to dark blue-green, coral-red to rose, to white. Brown, then rose shades again, brown, green, greenish-white, and again to blue-green, which makes such a dark accent in the jagged lines.

At the sides there is more red shading to rose, deep cream to cream-white and some of the same blue-green as in the centre. The front of the chasuble is much narrower but made up in much the same way except that the colours are brighter and there are no separate sections of different embroidery.

This chasuble is of extraordinary interest in that it appears at first glance to have been constructed from cleverly dove-tailed fragments, the main part worked in Hungarian point, with insets in Florentine stitch, This, however, is not the case, for on close inspection it will be seen that there is no break in the canvas between the two kinds of stitchery, both being used even in the narrow centre panel. This juxtaposition of the two stitches shows to perfection their different effect on the design, particularly the absence of any subsidiary pattern in the areas of Florentine stitch. It would be extremely interesting to know the reason for such a peculiar experiment. (COOPER UNION MUSEUM)

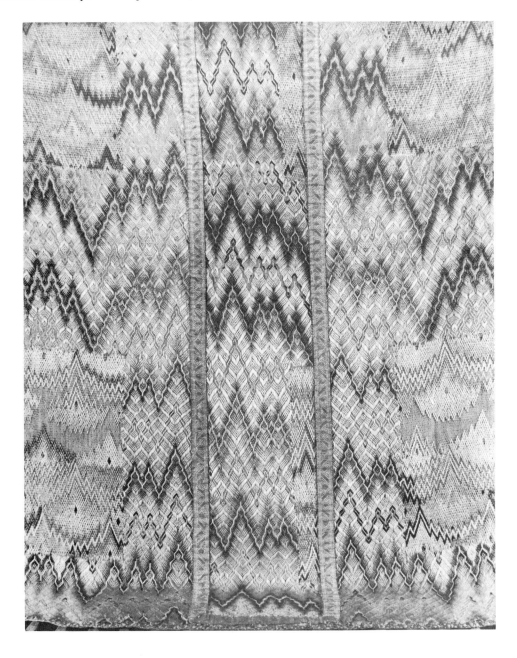

Parham Park, Sussex, is richly endowed with Florentine embroidery of great historical importance—two sets of embroidered wall curtains, the earliest probably unique, already referred to on p. 35, and the other in Hungarian point in an unusually bold festoon design, p. 56, as well as a complete set of bed curtains and valances, and a Queen Anne day-bed.

The Hungarian point hangings which lavishly decorate the Green Ante-Room cover one wall. The set of nine curtains, believed to date from the time of Charles II (1660–85), is thought to be of English workmanship. The festoon design with a flame line in silk and wool is exceedingly handsome. The 20″ wide canvas which includes a 5″ border has two festoons, caught up by a bow knot, fitting across the whole of each width. These are worked alternately in deep blue and a rich, fairly bright, but not harsh, red against a gold silk grounding based on Hungarian stitch, the gold deeper in some panels than in others. As often happens colour changes occur indiscriminately, presumably when one batch of dyed thread had been used up. The hangings are joined into three pieces, 110″ x 64″, 110″ x 100″, 90″ x 40″. The border on each narrow strip masks all joins in the pattern which follows-on in alternating colours over the whole great area, except in one or two places where interrupted by repairs; yet such is the over-all richness that all mistakes in the design are not at first noticed.

On the magnificent bed in the Great Chamber are four meticulously worked curtains, three top valances and three mattress valances which could well be the most perfect example of Hungarian point flame pattern in existence today. They are worked in silk and wool, the colours shaded in regular repeat, with negligible dye variation, ranging through greyish brown, oyster, a little dark blue to deepen the adjacent brown, soft shades of pink, yellow and green all blending together most subtly to give a general effect of cream, pink and chocolate. The narrow canvas, about $9\frac{1}{2}$″ wide, each strip containing two zigzags, involved much joining. A narrow border dis-

54

guises each seam; generally two zigzags and a border make up one strip, but occasionally a strip is bordered on both sides while its neighbour has none. This little border must have been very irritating to work with its frequent changes in colour and from wool to silk thread, yet even here great uniformity obtains. All the valances have an elaborately shaped edge carefully neatened with fine cord. Even this edge, which might be supposed fragile, also remains in good condition. The whole effect is very beautiful.

Colour arrangement:
 pink silk
 soft shades rust wool
 black ⎫
 yellow ⎪
 white ⎬ silk
 yellow ⎪
 black ⎭
 soft shades greyish brown wool
   getting lighter towards
 oyster silk
 1 line dark blue wool
 1 line brown wool
 soft pink wools getting lighter
   towards
 light pink silk
 green silk
 yellow silk
 green silk
 repeat pink silk

Bed in the Great Chamber, Parham Park, Sussex. Four curtains, three top valances and three mattress valances in Flame design worked in Hungarian point. (COURTESY OF THE HON. MRS. CLIVE PEARSON AND *Country Life*)

E2 type, 2 long, 2 short

FLORENTINE EMBROIDERY

The Queen Anne walnut day-bed, 5'8" x 2'1", with a scroll end has a fitting squab (loose cushion), worked in wool Hungarian point in an 8" flame design on 11" width canvas, the remaining 3" being a cross stitch border of scallop pattern. Colour shades through deep fawn, two rows of red, pale fawn, pale blue, deeper blue, fawn, blue-green and is then repeated with blue and blue-green alternating. A matching bolster-shaped pillow lies at the bed head.

Wall hangings in Charles II Room, Parham Park, probable date 1660–1685

Colour arrangement:
1 row brown wool
3 rows cream silk
1 row pale green silk
7 rows shading green to dark blue wool
1 row brown wool
7 rows shading dark
   to light blue-green wool

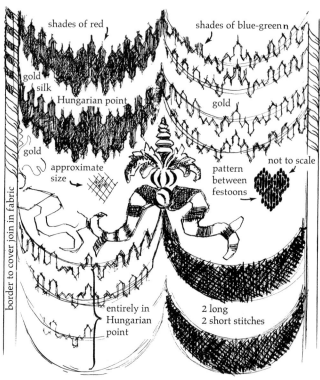

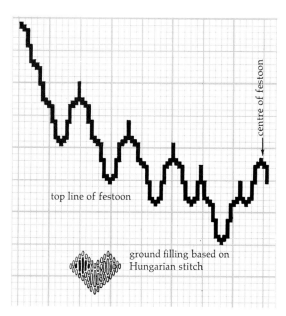

top line of festoon

ground filling based on
Hungarian stitch

PART II | *Techniques*

1. CANVAS

Single thread canvas used for Florentine stitch and Hungarian point embroidery is obtainable in various widths and threads to one inch, from 14 threads, which is fairly coarse, 16, 18, 20, 23, 24, to 28 which is very fine.

The number of threads to one inch in other fabrics which may be used is given here for comparison, and is only an approximate guide because texture and firmness of weave also affect the choice of material on which to work, for example, a 28 thread canvas appears very fine and does in fact permit more detailed work than a 30 thread even-weave material.

	Threads to 1″	*Manufacturer*
"Lauder" linen gauze	33	Old Glamis
"Willow" cross stitch material	30	Dryad
Even-weave linen	25, 28, 29	Glenshee (Richmond Bros.)
Norland openweave linen	22	Dryad
Coarse Willow	18	Dryad
Linen, various	13–19	Old Glamis
Embroidery fabrics, various	17–19	Glenshee

2. SUITABLE FABRICS OTHER THAN CANVAS

When Florentine stitch in any of its numerous forms is to be used as an open design, in lines or a spot arrangement, and not as on canvas, a close filling, the material on which the embroidery is worked shares in the colour scheme. Almost any even-weave material can be used and other fairly loosely woven fabrics where it is possible to count the threads.

Coarse Willow cross stitch material in natural, and Willow embroidery fabric in several colours, are much softer to handle than fine canvas. Glenshee mercerised cottons are of similar weight and Glenshee even-weave linens with a bright sheen, available in several widths and colours, are excellent to use.

Hardanger cloth with threads woven in pairs, is obtainable in white, natural and several colours; it has only one slight disadvantage in that warp and weft threads are not exactly of the same thickness so that a design becomes a little longer one way than the other. If the embroidery is worked in one direction no problem arises.

Norland openweave linen and Lauder linen gauze generally used for drawn fabric work may at first sight appear uncompromising material, but it proves a very pleasant ground on which to work in wool, stranded cotton and Sylko perlé (pearl cotton). Threads withdrawn from the material itself can be used for drawing the threads together if pulled (drawn) fabric work is introduced for further variety. This type of linen does not lose its shape unless carelessly handled; however, only a reasonably experienced needlewoman will attempt experimental work of this nature.

Fine flannel and dress weight woollens can be used only if the threads in the weave are distinguishable. Some Scandinavian furnish-

60

ing fabrics, especially those made in Finland, are almost like woollen gauze, and evoke new ideas in the field of Florentine embroidery.

3. THREADS

WOOL   Appleton's Crewel wool
Penelope Crewel wool, W. Briggs
Various 2 and 3 ply knitting wools and Angora wool
"Anchor" Tapisserie wool
Beehive Tapestry wool
Appleton's Tapestry wool
Kelim wool, similar in weight to double knitting

COTTON   Clark's Stranded cotton
Clark's Coton à Broder
Clark's "Anchor" Soft
Dewhurst's Sylko Perlé or Pearl Cotton No. 5
D. M. C. Stranded cotton
D. M. C. Sylko Perlé or Pearl Cotton No. 5

SILK   Unfortunately nothing has yet replaced Filoselle which is no longer manufactured. Floss silk is obtainable, but is so difficult to handle on any but the finest canvas that it may be disregarded by all but the most experienced needlewomen.

4. NEEDLES

FOR EMBROIDERY
    Tapestry   blunt tip, large eye, 24 (small)–13 (very large)
                 24 is suitable for all fine canvases
                 22 can be used on an 18 thread to 1″ canvas
FOR MAKING UP
    Sharps   No. 8 is recommended for general use.

5. RELATIONSHIP OF THREAD TO FABRIC

Canvas mesh and thread thickness must be considered simultaneously. If possible, experiments should be made on several different fabrics before work is begun. Threads of the same thickness need not be used throughout a design, but any change in thickness should be deliberate and purposeful, contributing to the texture of the work. While it is good that everyone should experiment, one rule must be observed . . . when canvas is used the mesh must be completely covered. Different makes of wool vary in their spinning; some are quite even and can be used one piece at a time; others equally good, may be uneven and should therefore be used double so that slight variations in thickness counteract one another.

Stranded cottons may be used 3, 4, or 6 strands at a time according to need. Sylko Perlé (Pearl cotton) can be used only if it fills the canvas mesh; on even-weave linen it is a successful contrast to stranded cotton.

Three ply knitting wool tends to work up thicker than crewel wool and if used on the same piece of embroidery, gives a different height and texture.

On fabrics other than canvas, which by their nature contribute to the finished work, all threads to be used must be tested for their appearance. They should lie smoothly together to give an even surface.

6. COLOUR CHOICE; CARE OF THREADS

Threads are available in a wide colour range. Their combined total surpasses the needs of any embroideress today. In the "Boat" panel 45 shades were used and in the "Owl" 13 shades, but in more orthodox designs 14 could easily be enough, allowing for 7 shades each of two colours.

Colours can, unwisely, be chosen from a shade card, which, while indicating the range, shows too small a piece to be of much use and the colours cannot be tested against each other. Even a selection of skeins in the hand can be deceptive; in the example (p. 91) pink and grey looked much more attractive in the skein; when actually worked, their tone contrast proved to be too great.

Colours must, without exception, be chosen in daylight; any form of artificial lighting plays strange tricks with both colour and tone. However, since much work will be done in artificial light, it is essential to see that colours are securely numbered . . . number tags too easily come adrift. A container made from a long band of linen or improvised from a strip of sheet, with a wide piece of tape stapled at 1″ intervals along the centre, makes a satisfactory cover for threads. If these are arranged in shade order with each number written on the tape, confusion can be avoided. Any odd usable lengths of thread should, when cut from the work, be slipped at once through their appropriate compartment. When using a finely graded colour range, it is quite impossible to distinguish single threads by any light other than daylight.

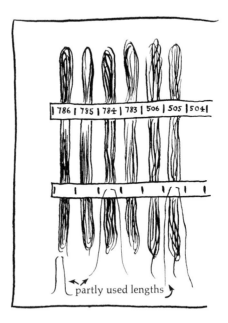

partly used lengths

Colour schemes must always be considered with their setting and use clearly in mind. Within the available wide range of threads deep rich colour schemes are as easily created as those which are very light and delicate, or softly subdued. Threads nowadays are normally fast colour. If only one thread in a subtle colour scheme fades to a different tone, many hours' work are wasted. Colour schemes in historical examples are not always easy to assess because fading has taken place at different rates. Generally blues, greens and yellows of the 17th and 18th century have faded very little whereas purple and in particular, the pink shades, have often changed to very lovely mushroom tones unobtainable at that time. While contemporary trends will always affect our choice of a colour scheme, a worthwhile piece of embroidery is not finished in a day, and the hours of work expended will only be justified if what we have made will endure for many years and has a lasting quality unaffected by the tides of fashion.

7. DESIGN

A glance through Part III will give some idea of the range of patterns in Florentine embroidery design. This is by no means an exhaustive collection. The slightest variations lead to other patterns; in fact, possibilities are almost infinite.

The patterns, however, do seem to fall into certain groups, some of which are more suited than others to present day use. On the whole the smaller, more compact, groundings are easier to live with than the huge repeats of the 17th and 18th centuries.

PLACING THE DESIGN ON THE FABRIC

If a traditional design is chosen, the position of the first line on the fabric can be worked out by counting; thereafter, row suc-

III.

LEFT: Italian 17th century panel in Florentine stitch, 4.2 step, worked with silk, mainly shades of soft blue and yellow, on linen canvas. A little cross, satin and slanting Gobelin stitch can be found in the motifs, a stylised rose, star and fleur de lys, whose shape subdivides the ground into diamonds.

BELOW: A vanity bag embroidered by the author (see page 142)

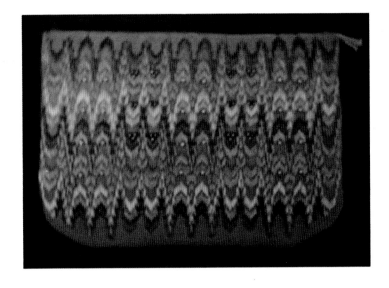

ceeds row and the sole guide needed is a small pencil sketch with thread colours recorded on it. This sounds simple enough, but it may in fact take a little time to establish the exact position of motifs in a piece of work like the hexagonal cushion on p. 127.

Even with the help of graph paper, variations in design are not always easy to work out correctly.

Florentine stitch has, in the past, frequently been used with other stitches. The modern approach to this aspect of the work can be found in Part IV and Part V.

8. TEXTURE

The regular 4.2 step gives a monotonous texture and interest depends entirely on the colour arrangement and on the introduction of different threads. Historically, this fact was appreciated. In the familiar carnation pattern, silk used in contrast to wool, either in part of the background or part of the motif, or in outlining the main shape, does much to alleviate the stitch's monotony. (See colour plate II, Alexander chair) The chief 'break through' in the combination of texture and colour came with the joint evolution of Hungarian ground and the 'flame' design, and the appearance of the subsidiary pattern which surely was at first accidental. (See V. & A. altar cloth p. 50.)

The importance of texture in design should not be underrated. There are no hard and fast rules to follow. In the napkin ring (p. 124) a smooth texture contrasts with the homespun cloth. The hexagonal cushion could have been worked with certain rows in a thicker or shiny thread. Such decisions are a matter of personal choice, but if in doubt, it is wiser not to strive too hard, too obviously, for the unusual effect. (See also Part V, Modern Design.)

65

9. FRAMES

Florentine stitch, being worked on the straight thread, does not need to be mounted in a frame, the use of which tends to immobilise the embroideress. Though essential for some kinds of canvas work in which certain stitches pull the canvas diagonally, a frame is all too often used for some imaginary prestige value. Work, carefully folded or better still, rolled, keeps in shape for as long as any piece of embroidery should take to do. Stretching over damp blotting paper (See p. 70) or pressing face downwards into a soft blanket brings the work to pristine freshness.

No frame has been used for any modern specimens in this book.

10. WORKING METHOD

Florentine patterns are based on an upright stitch; the line pattern depends on the length of stitch, length of step and the number of stitches in each step.

A stitch passing over 8 threads of canvas can be counted a long stitch; too many such, unless the thread is well chosen, will make a flimsy piece of work. Steps over 4, back 2, and 6.3 or 6.1 are more practical. Alternatively too short a stitch with very thick thread makes a hard lumpy fabric and too thick a thread also suffers during its passage to and fro, being frayed and roughened, which again results in untidy, uneven embroidery.

A Victorian woman, writing in 1842,* tells us "The needleful of wool should be short, both on account of soiling and impoverish-

* *Handbook of Needlework* by Miss Lambert published by John Murray 1842.

ing as it passes through the canvas, and a very small portion only should be passed through the eye of the needle. Finishing off on the same spot should always be avoided". For comfort wool should be

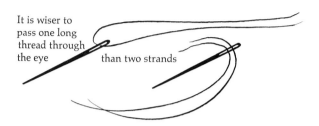

It is wiser to pass one long thread through the eye than two strands

about 16″ long and it is wise to move its position in the eye of the needle two or three times to avoid weakening the wool in one place. Doubled wool (above) should be cut to allow a 16″ working length. The loop in the eye may wear slightly but this will be cut away in any case when the thread is finished off. Two threads through the eye pass less easily through the mesh. There is no place for securing the beginning of the first thread until this piece has been used; therefore, to prevent the first stitches from slipping, the thread should begin with a knot at a point about 2″ from the first stitch. Immediately this first thread has been used and its final end darned into the back of the work, the knot must be snipped off and the end darned in. As work progresses there is more room for securing the ends which must not accumulate in one place as this causes an uneven surface.

Some Florentine patterns such as those in B group have much more wool on the back than do others, for example those in E group. This should be considered when making a design; a very thick stitch will produce a too bulky small article whereas the same stitch may be advantageous on a stool top where additional padding cannot come amiss.

The need to balance thickness of thread with mesh of canvas cannot be emphasised too often. If the canvas is not entirely covered, 67

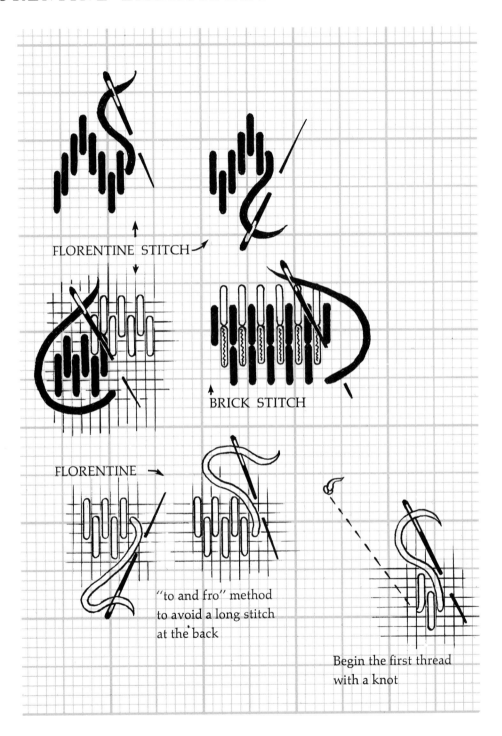

FLORENTINE STITCH

BRICK STITCH

FLORENTINE

"to and fro" method
to avoid a long stitch
at the back

Begin the first thread
with a knot

flecks of light mesh showing through between the stitches disturb the design, prove that the thread is not thick enough and consequently that the work will not wear well. Canvas and wool together have great endurance, proved by some 17th and 18th century work in use within living memory, and while we may not expect our work to last 200 or 300 years, we should do our best to make it technically sound.

11. GENERAL PRACTICAL NOTES

1. On canvas protect the edges by oversewing or binding, to prevent fraying.

2. Do not cut curves or diagonal edges until work is finished; a rectangular piece of canvas keeps in shape.

3. Allow a generous margin beyond the design.

4. On materials other than canvas a guide line tacked to indicate the final shape may be helpful in determining where to finish or adjust a row of stitches.

5. Lay threads side by side to make certain of their colour relationship to one another; write down their order as a precaution against mistakes which easily occur in artificial light.

6. Keep a needle threaded with each colour.

7. Use short lengths of stranded cotton and Sylko perlé to avoid losing their gloss, and short lengths of wool to avoid weakening the fibres by too frequent passage through the canvas.

8. When making up work, always oversew canvas from the right side, between every embroidery stitch, with cotton which sinks invisibly into the embroidery.

12. STRETCHING FINISHED CANVAS WORK

A completed piece of embroidery on canvas will need stretching to its original size, in spite of the fact that it may not have taken up noticeably while it has been worked. Stretching should be done by placing several sheets of clean blotting paper on a clean board, important because stain can percolate up through the fabric. The embroidery is thumb-tacked to the board, right side up, beginning in one corner, pulling very hard along one edge while keeping it parallel with the edge of the board; the adjacent edge is pinned next, then the two other sides. If the whole process is done patiently, working round several times, pulling outwards a little more each time, the pins will not bounce out too often, a tantalising occurrence. This task is hard on the fingers and there is no easy way out. To ensure that the work is pulled true, with right-angled corners, the edge of the fabric should be measured from the edge of the board with a gauge. When all is well, water is carefully trickled on to the blotting paper, *behind the embroidery,* until saturation point is reached. The front of the embroidery itself must not get wet. About 24 hours should elapse before the work, quite dry, and beautifully freshened, is released.

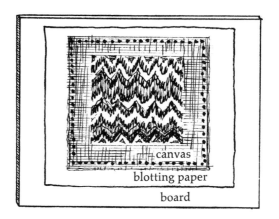

13. FRESHENING EMBROIDERY WHICH HAS NOT BEEN WORKED ON CANVAS

Florentine embroidery which has not been worked on canvas should be placed face downwards on a blanket and gently pressed from the wrong side, easing the fabric outwards from the center. This method was used for the beaded vanity bag (p. 143) and the apron (p. 72), both worked on "Willow" cross stitch material, and for the owl (p. 151) worked on loosely woven linen.

14. MAKING UP FINISHED WORK

Surprising though it may seem, a good embroideress is not necessarily a good needlewoman when it comes to making up her embroidery. Excellent work can easily be ruined and made to appear clumsily amateurish if careful sewing technique is not completely followed through to the end. To many of us this final stage is tedious. Attaching other material to canvas must be done by hand, sewing between every thread of the mesh, with small straight oversewing stitches, always working from the right side because the work is too thick to be turned inside out.

In Part V details are given of the different stages involved in making up several of the examples created for this book.

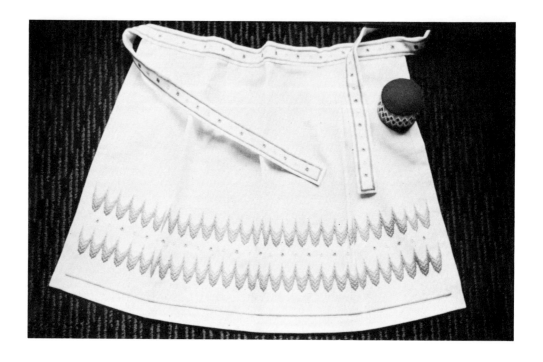

A child's apron (directions on page 144) and a detail of the border

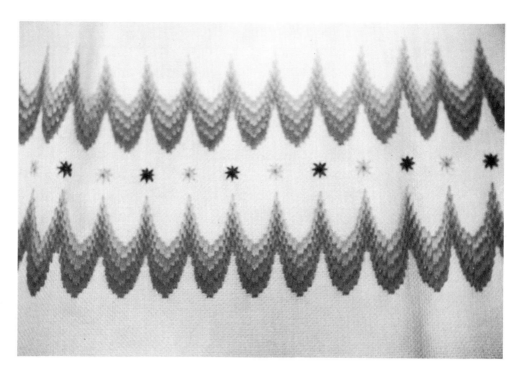

72

PART III

Diagrams of
Patterns in
Florentine Stitch
and
Hungarian Point

INTRODUCTION

Although these patterns fall into fairly clearly defined groups a slight alteration in either length of stitch or number of stitches in each step can change the pattern from one type to another. Some of the smaller designs, particularly those which do not have a continuous line running through them, could equally well be considered as "groundings" a term for which it is difficult to find a true definition. (See page 101)

A1. UNBROKEN LINES

Same number of stitches in each step
Same length step
Same length stitch

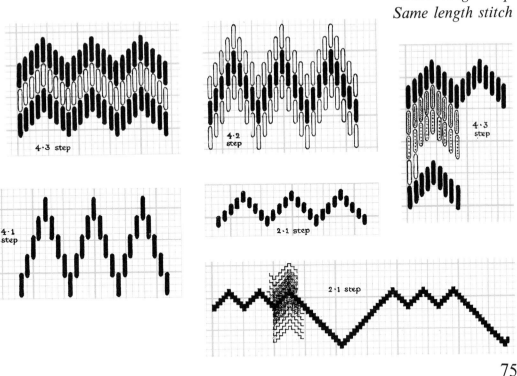

FLORENTINE EMBROIDERY

A1. UNBROKEN LINES

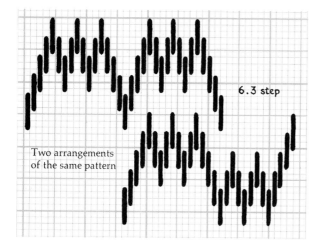

6.3 step

Two arrangements
of the same pattern

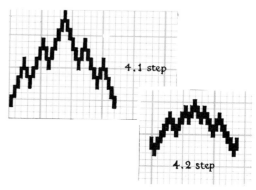

4.1 step

4.2 step

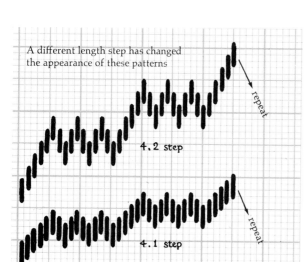

A different length step has changed
the appearance of these patterns

4.2 step

repeat

4.1 step

repeat

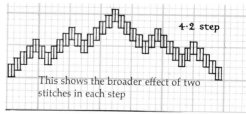

4·2 step

This shows the broader effect of two
stitches in each step

4·2 step

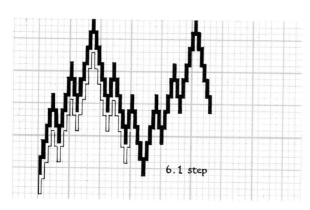

6.1 step

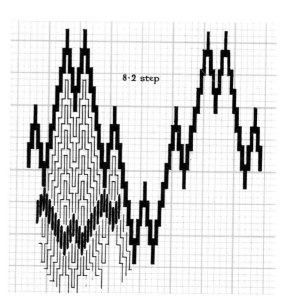

8·2 step

DIAGRAMS OF PATTERNS

A1. UNBROKEN LINES

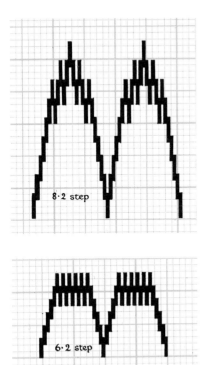

8·2 step

6·2 step

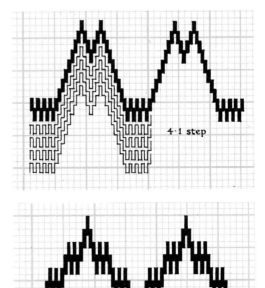

4·1 step

6·2 step

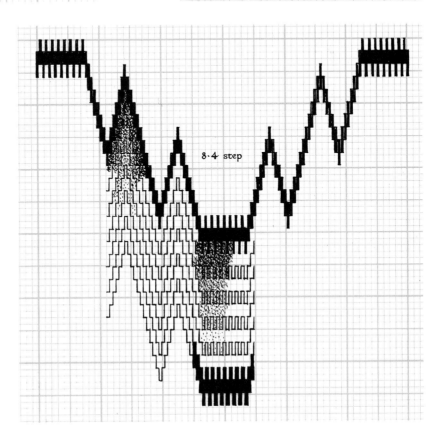

8·4 step

A2. PARTLY BROKEN LINES
Same number of stitches in each step
Same length step
Same length stitch

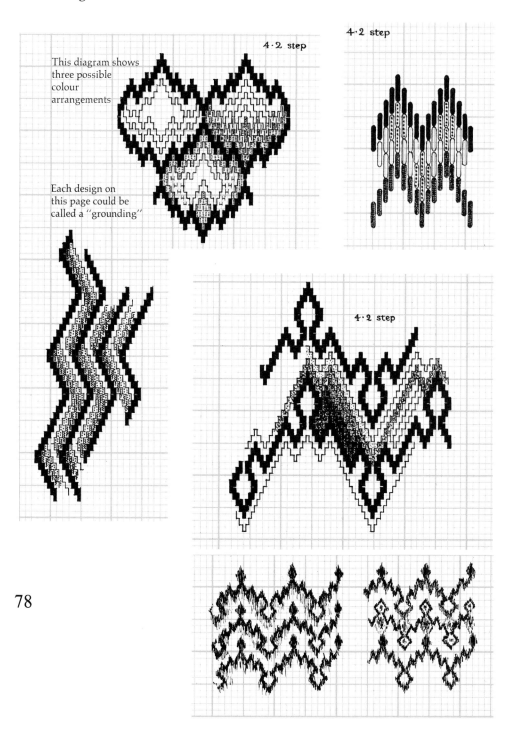

This diagram shows three possible colour arrangements

4·2 step

4·2 step

Each design on this page could be called a "grounding"

4·2 step

78

A2. PARTLY BROKEN LINES

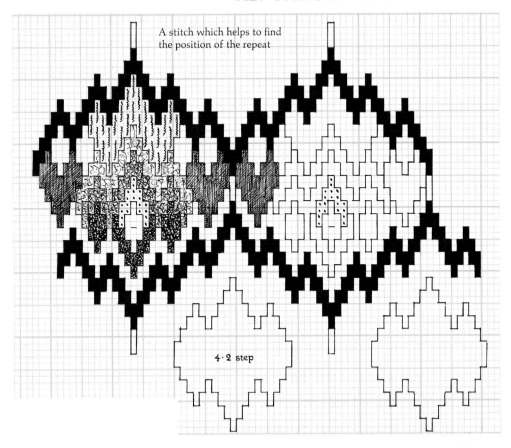

A stitch which helps to find
the position of the repeat

4·2 step

Sketch to show the
effect of a tone change
on alternate bands

A2. PARTLY BROKEN LINES

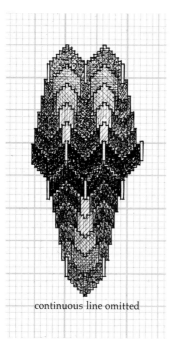

continuous line omitted

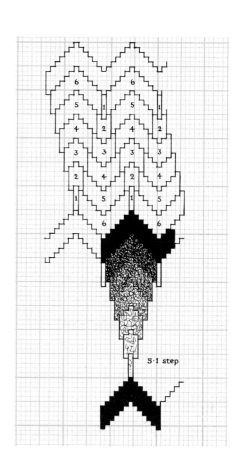

5·1 step

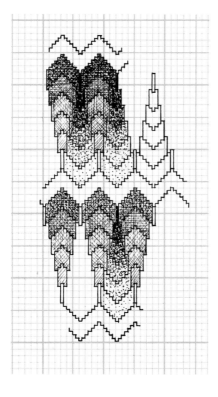

80

A3. BROKEN LINES

Same number of stitches in each step
Same length step
Same length stitch
These are also Groundings G2 type

"BASKET WEAVE"
PATTERNS

Each block represents
2 stitches

All 4·2 step

FLORENTINE EMBROIDERY

B1. UNBROKEN LINES
Variable number of stitches in each step
Same length step
Same length stitch

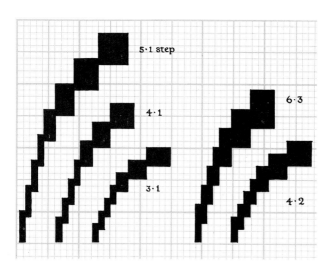

Group B patterns being akin to satin stitch, have much wool on the back. This should be taken into account when designing small articles. If the blocks of stitches are pulled too tightly, the mesh is exposed, a fact well known to the Victorians who exploited the horizontal stitch they darned in as a cover, sometimes only making matters worse by over-emphasising the line with too thick a thread or too strongly contrasting a colour.

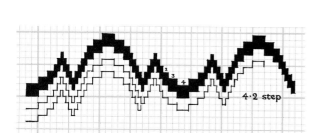

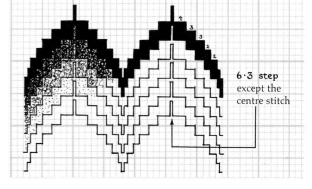

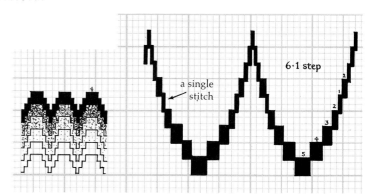

82

B1. UNBROKEN LINES

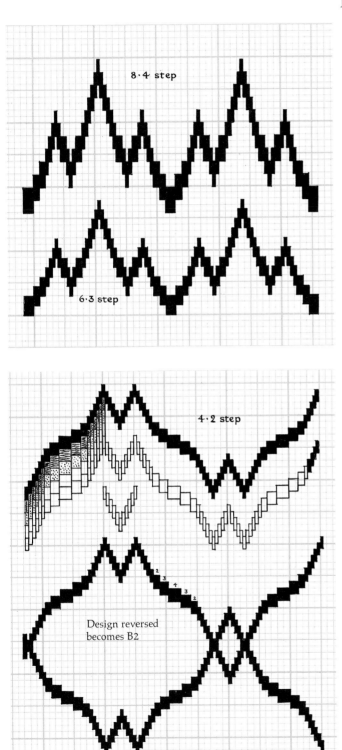

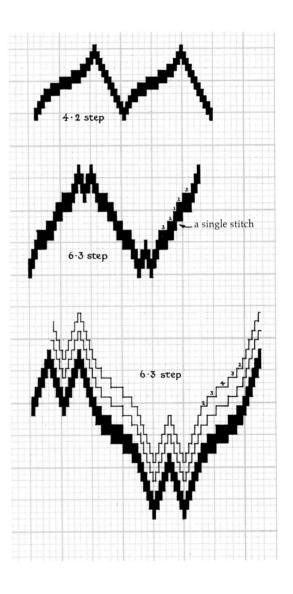

8·4 step

6·3 step

4·2 step

Design reversed
becomes B2

4·2 step

6·3 step

a single stitch

6·3 step

83

B1. UNBROKEN LINES

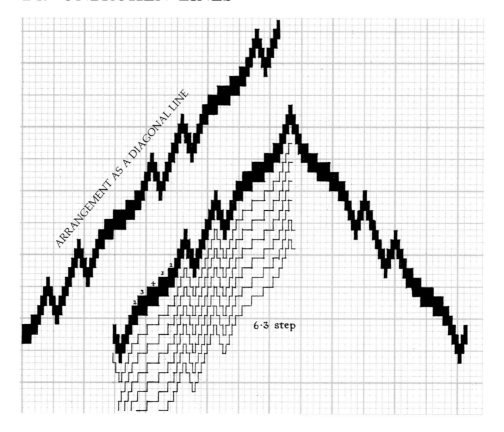

ARRANGEMENT AS A DIAGONAL LINE

6·3 step

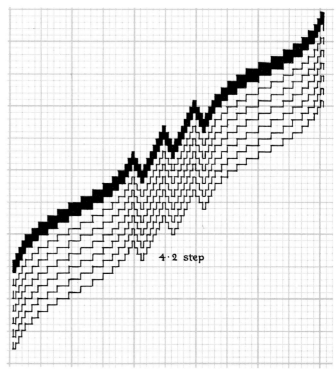

4·2 step

84

B1. UNBROKEN LINES

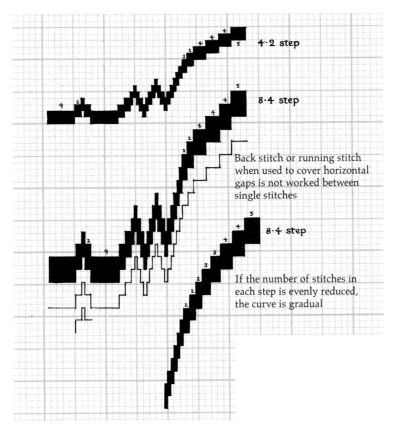

4·2 step

8·4 step

Back stitch or running stitch when used to cover horizontal gaps is not worked between single stitches

8·4 step

If the number of stitches in each step is evenly reduced, the curve is gradual

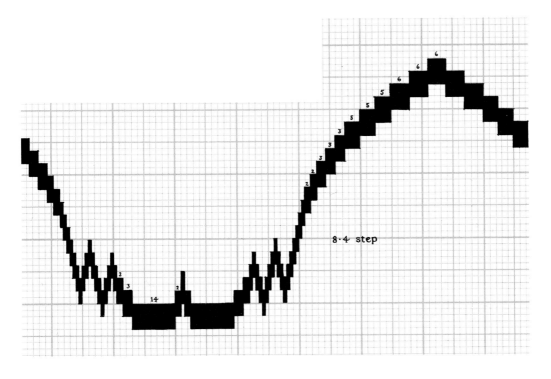

8·4 step

B1. UNBROKEN LINES

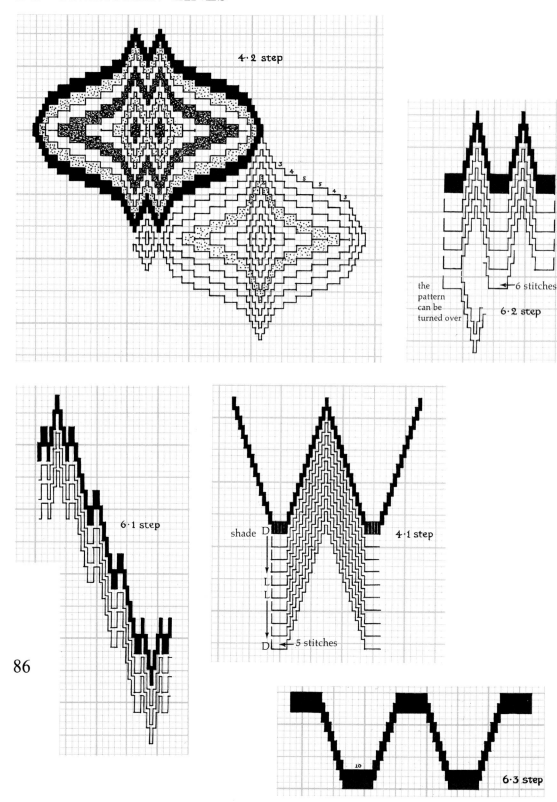

4·2 step

3
4
5
5
4
3

the
pattern
can be
turned over ← 6 stitches

6·2 step

6·1 step

shade D
L
L
DL ← 5 stitches

4·1 step

10

6·3 step

86

B1. UNBROKEN LINES

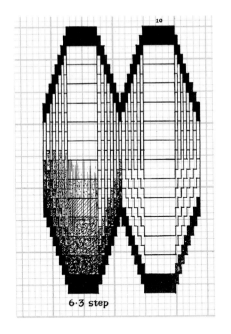

6·3 step

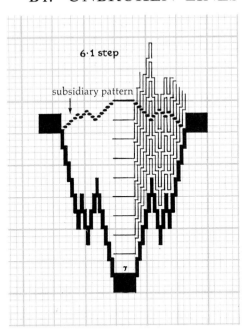

6·1 step

subsidiary pattern

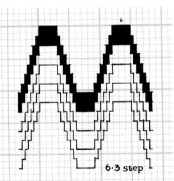

6·3 step

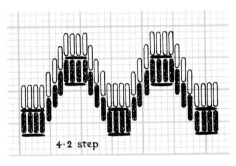

4·2 step

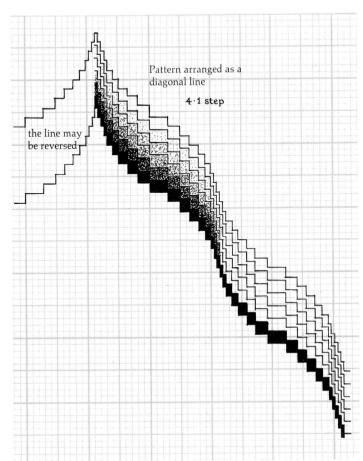

Pattern arranged as a
diagonal line

4·1 step

the line may
be reversed

B2. USUALLY *ONE* CONTINUOUS LINE, THE OTHER LINES BROKEN

Variable number of stitches in each step
Same length step
Same length stitch, except where an occasional small stitch is needed to make the pattern fit
All the smaller patterns could be called Groundings

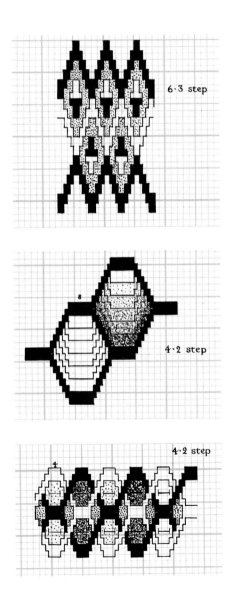

6·3 step

4·2 step

4·2 step

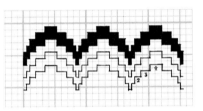

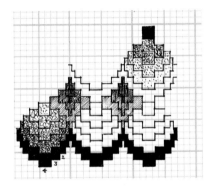

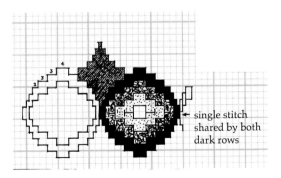

← single stitch shared by both dark rows

B2. USUALLY *ONE* CONTINUOUS LINE, THE OTHER LINES BROKEN

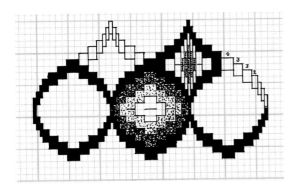

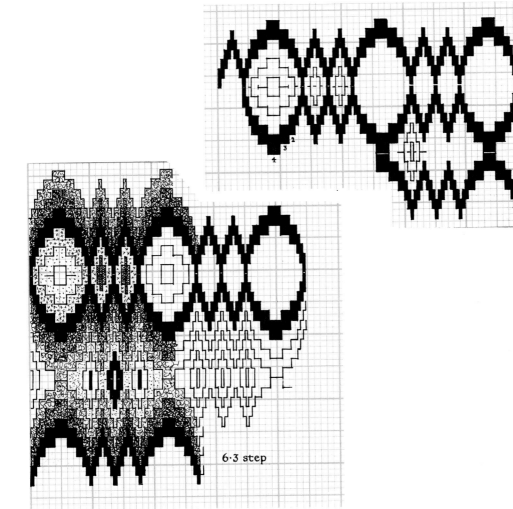

6·3 step

89

B2. USUALLY *ONE* CONTINUOUS LINE, THE OTHER LINES BROKEN

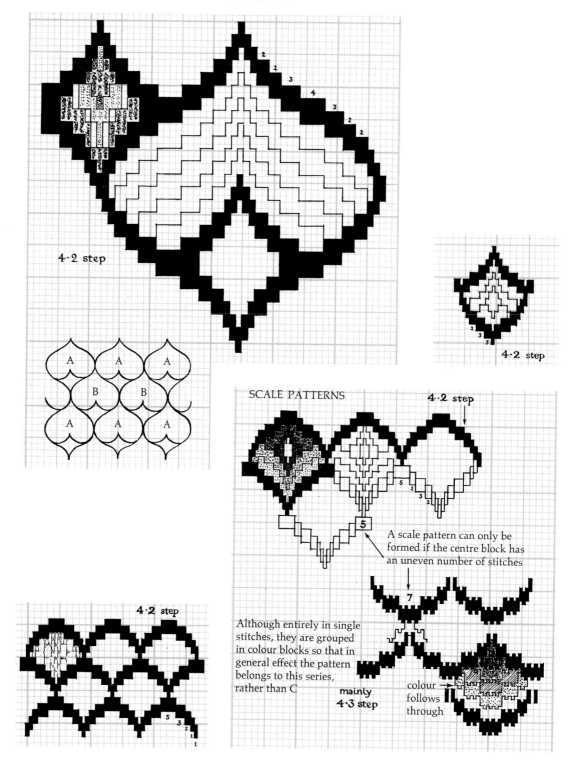

4·2 step

A A A
B B
A A A

4·2 step

4·2 step

SCALE PATTERNS 4·2 step

5

A scale pattern can only be formed if the centre block has an uneven number of stitches

7

Although entirely in single stitches, they are grouped in colour blocks so that in general effect the pattern belongs to this series, rather than C

mainly 4·3 step

colour → follows through

B2. USUALLY *ONE* CONTINUOUS LINE, THE OTHER LINES BROKEN

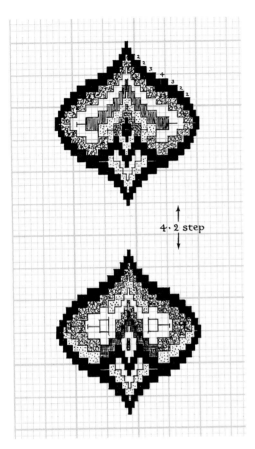

4·2 step

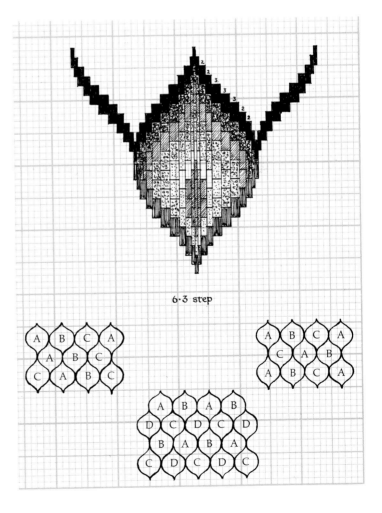

6·3 step

C.

Single stitches
Same length stitches
Different length step

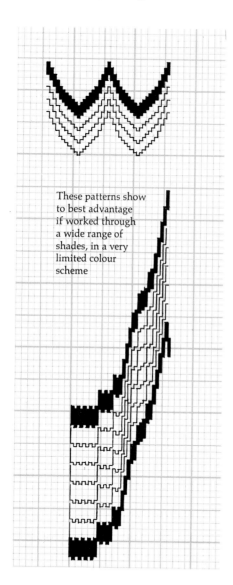

These patterns show
to best advantage
if worked through
a wide range of
shades, in a very
limited colour
scheme

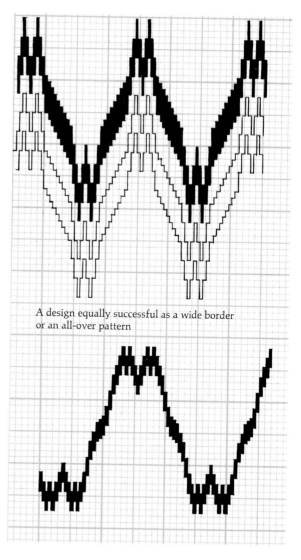

A design equally successful as a wide border
or an all-over pattern

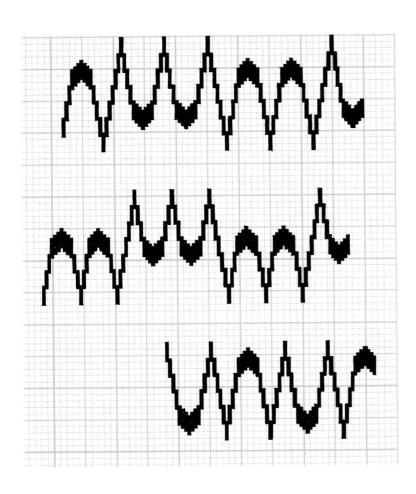

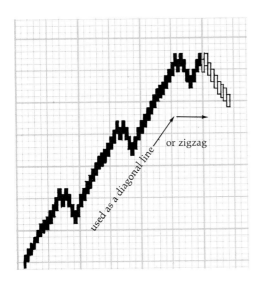

or zigzag

used as a diagonal line

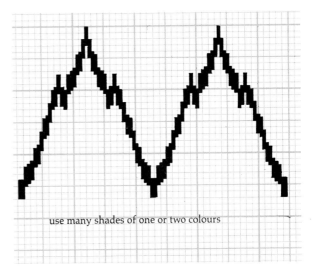

use many shades of one or two colours

C.

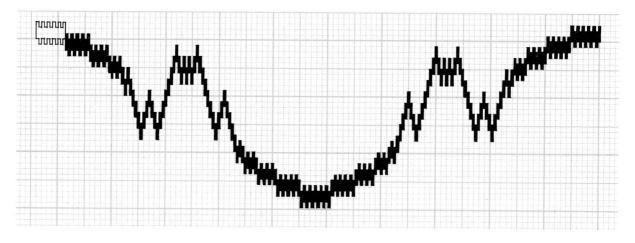

D.

Same number of stitches in each step
Varied length of step
Varied length stitch

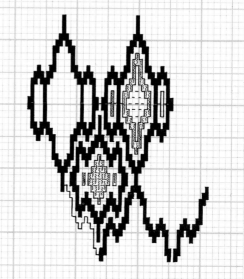

94

E1. HUNGARIAN POINT

One large stitch
Two small stitches

The term Hungarian Point is used to describe a particular method in Florentine embroidery. It is worked in rows of single stitches, in steps of 1 long, 2 short; 2 long 2 short; 1 long and 3 or more short. The patterns are exceedingly confusing to copy and to work, even when it is realised that a "1 long 2 short" line will repeat on the third line and a "1 long 3 short" pattern will repeat on the fourth line. In *drafting* it helps to remember that if a vertical line is followed, one long stitch comes in line with two or three short as the case may be. (below)

In historical examples the repeat is usually completely hidden by a wide range of tints spreading over many rows before these in turn repeat themselves.

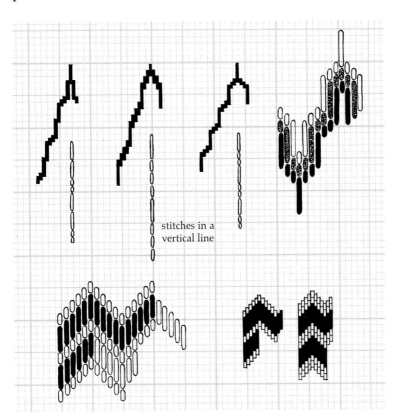

stitches in a
vertical line

E1. HUNGARIAN POINT

Another complication is the presence of a subsidiary pattern which appears somewhat mysteriously as the result of the shape of the main repeat line. This gives an interesting additional texture and further enriches already elaborate work.

Hungarian Point, to be seen at its best, must cover a very large area. Of all the Florentine embroideries this striking pattern is least suited to the present day home.

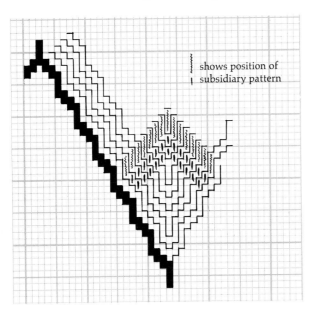

shows position of subsidiary pattern

96

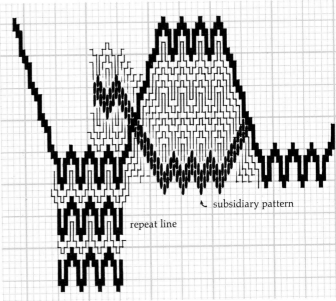

subsidiary pattern

repeat line

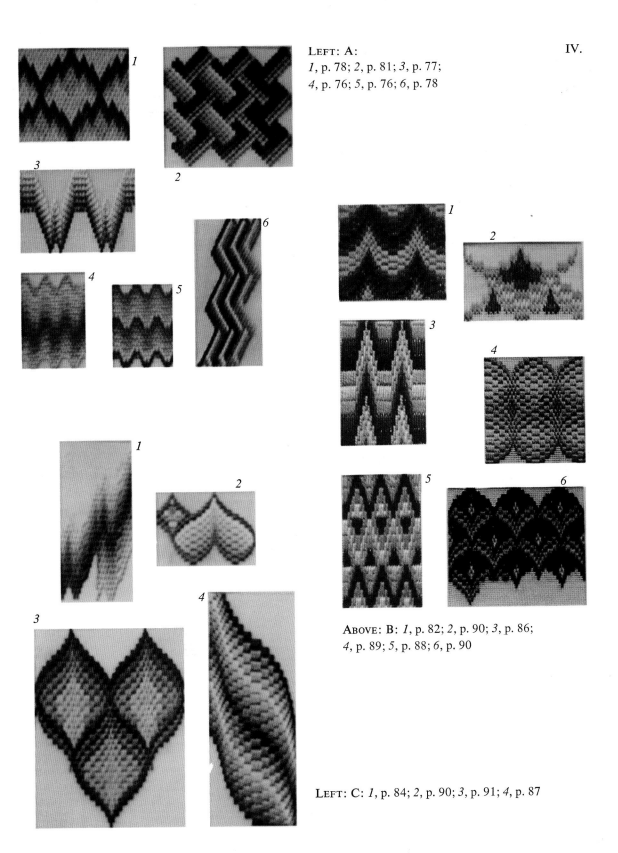

E2.

Two large stitches
Two small stitches

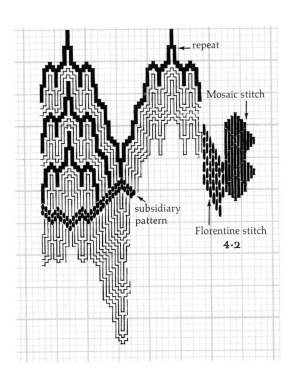

repeat

Mosaic stitch

subsidiary
pattern

Florentine stitch

4·2

On the original the colours were used without regular repetition, eleven rows shaded blue from dark to light, three rows brown and gold, two white, three pink, seven fawn, brown, gold, brown, two white and eight shades of green. This resulted in the absolute disappearance of the true repeat in the pattern and it was not discovered until the cartoon was drawn. The subsidiary zigzag merely gave varied texture. The source of this design, an unfinished panel worked in filoselle on a soft canvas, with narrow dividing borders of mosaic stitch, is in all probability late 19th century work. Its purpose is unknown, but the softness of the cotton canvas suggests that it was intended as a hanging.

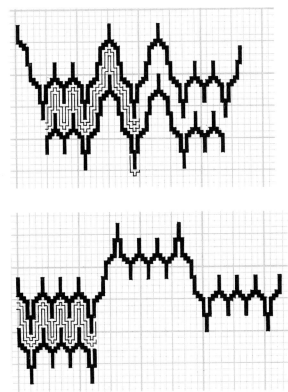

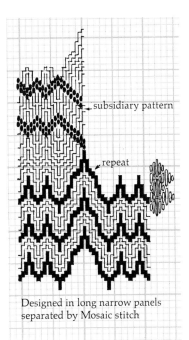

subsidiary pattern

repeat

Designed in long narrow panels
separated by Mosaic stitch

97

E2.

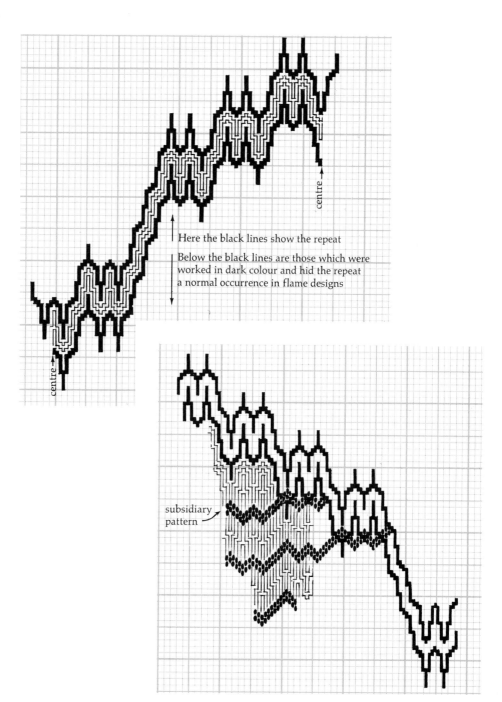

Here the black lines show the repeat

Below the black lines are those which were
worked in dark colour and hid the repeat
a normal occurrence in flame designs

centre →

centre →

subsidiary
pattern

DIAGRAMS OF PATTERNS

E3.

One large stitch
Two small stitches

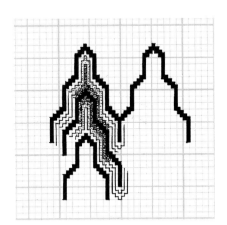
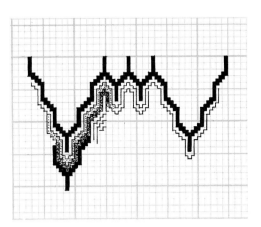

E4.

Other variations

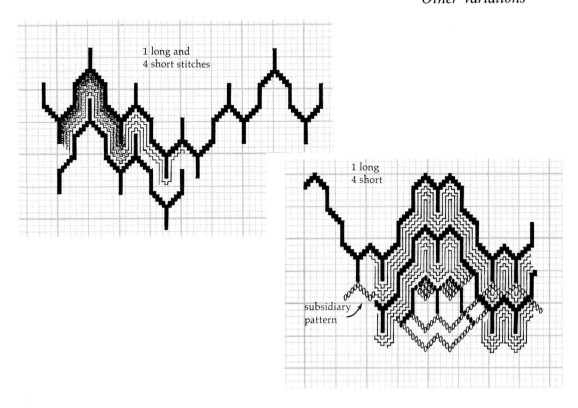

1 long and
4 short stitches

1 long
4 short

subsidiary
pattern

E4.

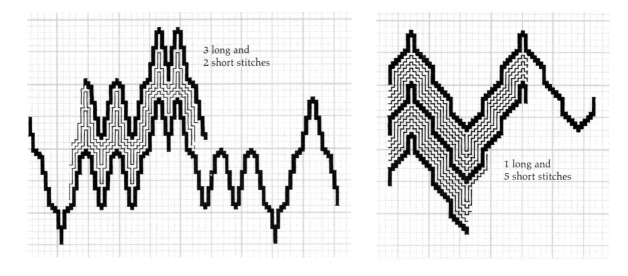

3 long and
2 short stitches

1 long and
5 short stitches

ANALYSIS CHART

	DIAGRAM TO SHOW THE MAIN VARIATIONS IN THE STEP ARRANGEMENT FOUND IN FLORENTINE PATTERNS					
	NUMBER OF STITCHES IN EACH STEP		LENGTH OF STITCH IN EACH STEP		LENGTH OF STEP IN EACH ROW	
	CONSTANT	VARIABLE	CONSTANT	VARIABLE	CONSTANT	VARIABLE
	A1		A1		A1	
	A2		A2		A2	
	A3		A3		A3	
		B1	B1		B1	
		B2	B2		B2	
	C		C			C
	D			D		D
based on Hungarian point	E1				E1	
	E2				E2	
	E3				E3	
	E4				E4	

GROUNDINGS

Grounding is the term in general use for a fairly small all-over pattern. We do not now simply mean background as does Miss Lambert, to quote again from her Victorian book, "It is curious that the grounding, one of the most particular parts of the work, should generally be deemed of such minor importance. Although a tedious and uninteresting process, yet when properly accomplished, it fully repays the trouble bestowed." No one involved in the intricacies of a Florentine grounding will find the occupation tedious. Since Florentine embroidery is normally concerned in covering a whole area, any distinction between what may be called the main field of design and a background pattern is purely arbitrary.

Many patterns found in groups A–E can also be considered groundings, particularly those which do not have continuous lines of colour running through them, but even this is no absolute criterion.

MAIN VARIATIONS IN THE STEP ARRANGEMENT IN GROUNDINGS

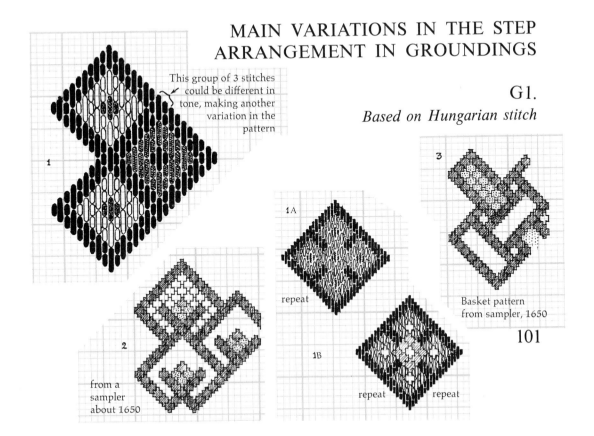

This group of 3 stitches could be different in tone, making another variation in the pattern

G1.

Based on Hungarian stitch

1

1A

repeat

3

Basket pattern from sampler, 1650

2

from a sampler about 1650

1B

repeat

repeat   repeat

101

FLORENTINE EMBROIDERY

G2.

Based on Florentine stitch,
4.2 step, with either one or
two stitches in a block

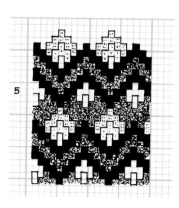

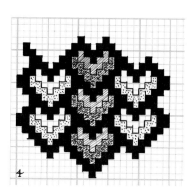

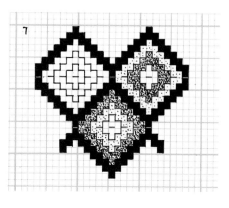

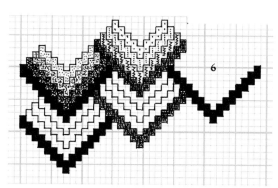

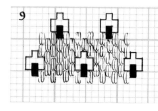

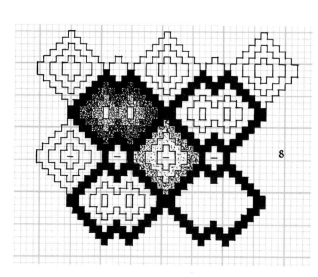

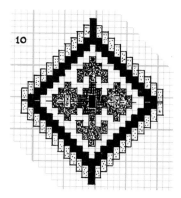

G2.

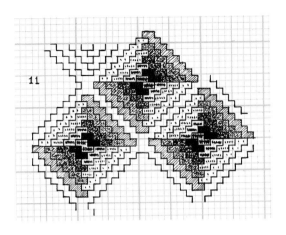

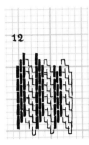

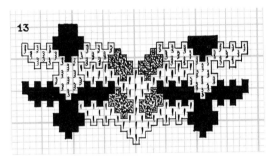

G3.

Based on Florentine stitch,
regular step, evenly divided,
6.3, 2.1, etc.

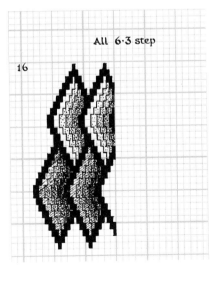

All 6·3 step

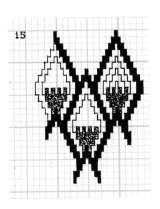

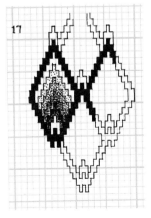

G3.

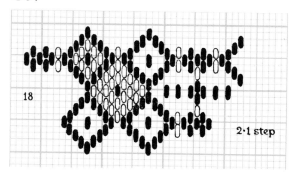

18

2·1 step

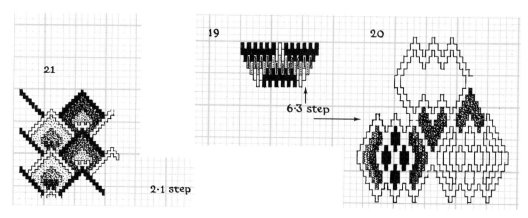

21

2·1 step

19

6·3 step

20

G4.

*Patterns with same length stitch
and variable number of
threads in each block*

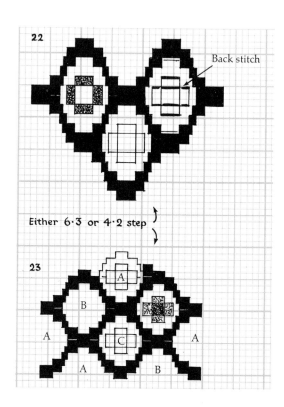

22

Back stitch

Either 6·3 or 4·2 step

23

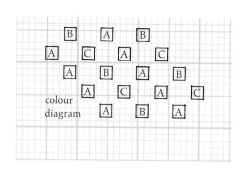

colour
diagram

G5.

*Patterns with variable length stitch
and same number of
stitches in each block*

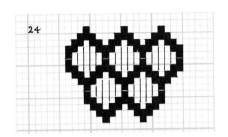

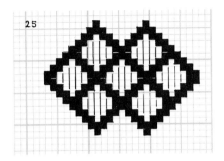

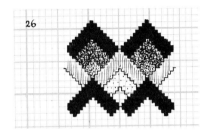

G6.

Other variations

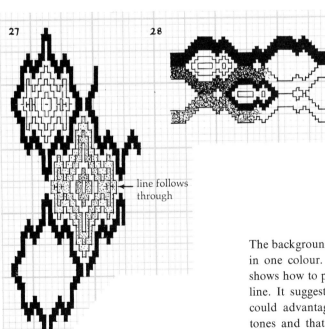

← line follows through

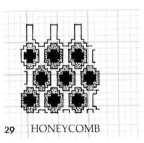

29   HONEYCOMB

The background in Honeycomb grounding is worked in one colour. The enlarged diagram on page 106 shows how to proceed after working one continuous line. It suggests, incidentally, that the background could advantageously be broken up into different tones and that new patterns would result from an arrangement of unbroken lines at intervals across the design.

G6.

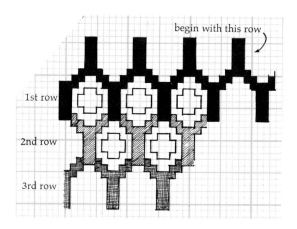

begin with this row

1st row

2nd row

3rd row

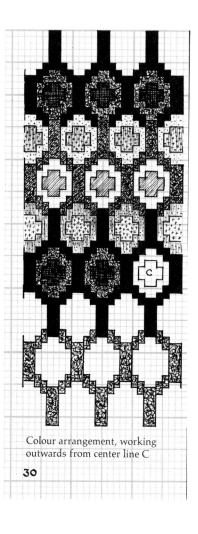

106

Colour arrangement, working
outwards from center line C

30

HONEYCOMB

Alternative colour scheme
emphasizing different
shapes in the pattern

31

G7.

Patterns based, even remotely,
on Hungarian Point—E group

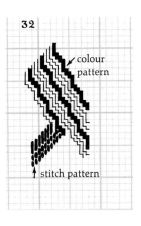

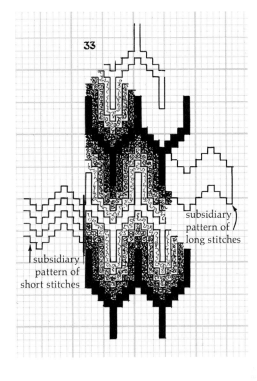

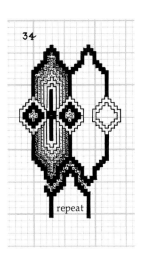

107

G7.

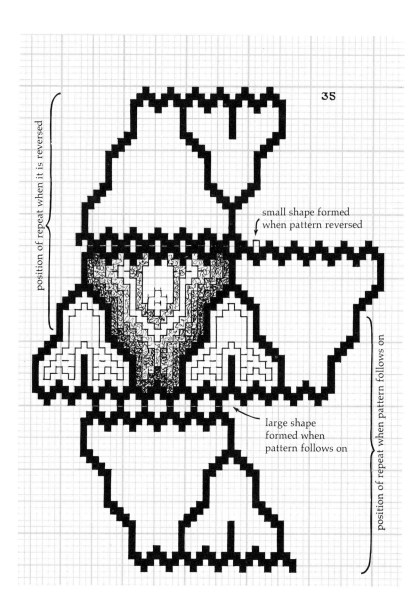

position of repeat when it is reversed

35

small shape formed
when pattern reversed

large shape
formed when
pattern follows on

position of repeat when pattern follows on

PART IV

Canvas Stitches which will link easily with Florentine Stitch and Hungarian Point

USEFUL ADJOINING STITCHES

As we have already seen on historical examples, stitches other than Hungarian, Florentine and Hungarian point were used in Florentine embroidery; tent, Byzantine, mosaic stitch and French knots played their part in large Italian floral designs. We have noticed too, that where patterns have not worked out accurately, or where the stitchery has abruptly been turned at a right angle, stray stitches have quite simply been fitted in to fill the spaces. Nowadays we are more selfconscious about technique.

In a pictorial or abstract design with Florentine merely one amongst many other stitches, the transition from one stitch to another may affect the design itself. Only a few stitches link easily into Florentine and Hungarian stitches. Among canvas stitches worked on the straight thread the most suitable are:—

Byzantine, brick, upright Gobelin, straight Gobelin, Parisian, Hungarian ground and satin.

Other stitches worked over the diagonal thread, tent, cross, rice and eyelet, will not pull the canvas out of shape if used with discretion, that is, over very small areas or, in the case of eyelet, as an isolated stitch.

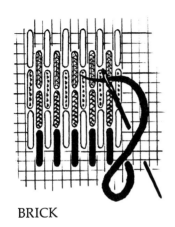

BRICK

HUNGARIAN

FLORENTINE EMBROIDERY

PARISIAN

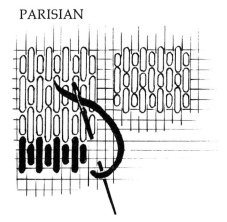

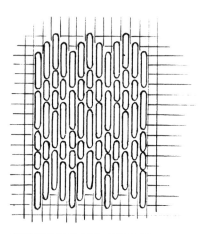

UPRIGHT GOBELIN

HUNGARIAN GROUND

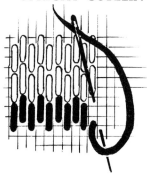

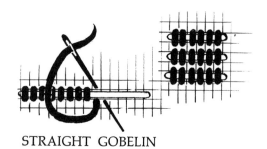

STRAIGHT GOBELIN

CROSS STITCH

Each cross must be
made separately;
each stitch must cross
in the same direction

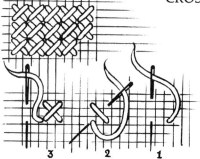

SATIN

DIAMOND EYELET

EYE STITCH

Back stitch may
be needed
to cover canvas

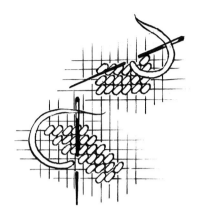

TENT STITCH

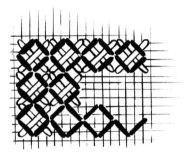

RICE STITCH

Work a ground of cross stitch; tie down each corner by working two horizontal rows of diagonal stitches

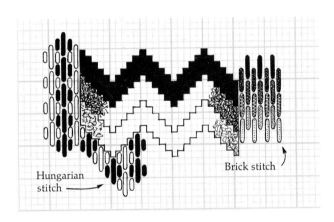

Hungarian stitch

Brick stitch

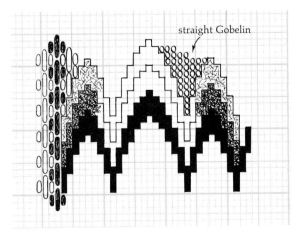

straight Gobelin

113

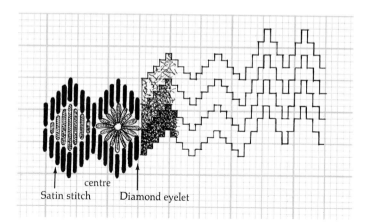

centre

Satin stitch   Diamond eyelet

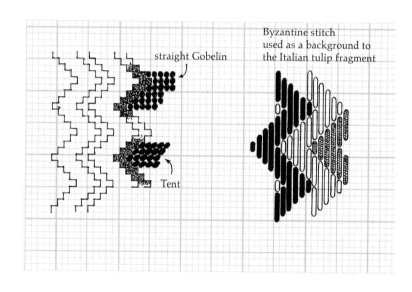

straight Gobelin

Tent

Byzantine stitch
used as a background to
the Italian tulip fragment

PART V

The Present Day Use of Florentine Embroidery

INTRODUCTION

The study of Florentine stitch and Hungarian point is but a fraction of the larger subject of canvas embroidery. The present day use of this can prove as stimulating to the designer as ever it did in the past. Certainly large hangings are unlikely to be needed, and even if they were, would require a corporate effort for their completion, but upholstery is within the scope of an individual embroideress, who can also make many small objects, each in a very short time. It is vitally important that the scale of pattern should be in accordance with the size of the article to be made; this, and the wise choice of colour and tone cannot be too often emphasised, and holds true for all canvas embroidery.

A design must always give the impression that it is an integral part of the object which has been made, that it has grown from the materials used and is not something afterwards applied. Today, with the widened range of suitable fabrics, many of them beautiful in both colour and texture, absolving us of the need to cover them completely, the designer can, within the limitations imposed by regular stitches, exploit these values and create unusual and individual work.

Two aspects of the use of Florentine stitch have not as yet been fully explored; the first, in pictorial design, and the second, in its relationship to materials other than canvas. Neither should be studied in isolation, and an attempt has been made in the succeeding pages to show the process by which designs may be evolved. The owl,

(p. 151) created from a design intended for canvas, developed instead on Norland open-weave linen, more freely than had been foreseen. The introduction of drawn fabric stitches in the background was not premeditated. On the body, patterns which began as Florentine stitch changed as work progressed. Such a liaison between mind, hand, fabric and thread can be likened to the unity which exists between an experienced horseman and his mount.

Designing comes easily to very few people; even the most fluent know that hiatus between one idea and the next, when it would seem that nothing new can ever be forthcoming. For most of us design involves considerable effort.

If we think of Florentine embroidery in terms of texture, as a varied means of covering a surface rather than as a series of zigzag lines, ideas may come more freely. With this in mind a study of modern French tapestries, particularly those of Jean Lurçat, can open up exciting vistas. His masterly treatment of feathers as a flat pattern, his angular shapes and unusual colour, are invigorating. From his work we learn that simplification does not mean monotony.

PRACTICAL NOTES

1. Ideas for design emanate from unexpected sources. In selection it must be remembered that shapes themselves should be simple, thus if inspiration comes from a prehistoric cave painting, that of a rhinoceros or a bison will adapt more successfully than a gazelle or giraffe because the former are essentially mass shapes while the latter are both linear.

2. Ideas for colour may be suggested by the leaves of a house plant, the subtle tones of driftwood, moss on a tree stump seen in the strange light of the rain forest, or in brilliant minerals with all their array of crystal formation.

118

3. Pattern ideas may come from rock strata in Yosemite, the convolutions of a shell, from the damp shore line on a rugged coast. To the alert eye all are potential design sources.

4. Most of the designs in Part V are based on straightforward stitch arrangements shown in Part III. Sometimes a small piece of pattern has been taken from a grounding and turned into a spot motif which can easily be traced back to the original. Other work has taken advantage of the varied shapes and adaptability of Florentine lines, and the ease with which they can be shaded. Where a working cartoon is not given, reference is made to the pattern's source.

5. For the more ambitious needlewoman who wishes to create her own designs, students' sketches are included to show how the impetus of one idea leads to another and the process by which it goes forward to a finished piece of pictorial work.

6. Objects, not illustrated, which could be embroidered in Florentine stitch or Hungarian point:

   1. Toilet seat cover
   2. Bathroom mat on rug canvas, worked in rug wool
   3. Small rug on coarse canvas, 14 threads to 1″
   4. Screen
   5. Bedhead
   6. Upholstery for chairs or small seats
   7. Top and sides of a "pouffe"

PINCUSHION

MATERIAL	Single thread white canvas 23 threads to 1″
	Felt for top and base
THREAD	Stranded cotton, blue, pink, white, yellow
	Sylko perlé No. 5 (Pearl cotton)
SIZE	$1\frac{1}{4}$″ deep, $2\frac{1}{4}$″ diameter
TO MAKE UP	Join the side seam, sewing from the right side with matching cotton. Fold the edges over, creasing firmly and snipping them (diag. 1). Cut two felt circles without turnings to fit exactly at each end. Place one piece of felt in position and pin edge to edge (diag. 2). With cotton to match the felt, sew between every thread of canvas. Use short lengths of cotton and pull tightly. Sew on the other end in the same way, partially stuffing the pincushion when $\frac{2}{3}$ sewn, adding fragments of stuffing as the gap closes.

DESIGN TYPE A2

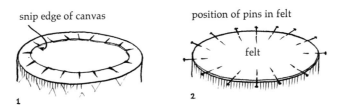

snip edge of canvas

position of pins in felt

felt

1

2

120

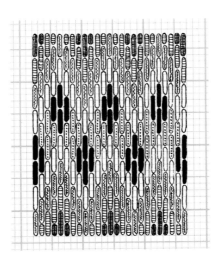

SCISSORS CASE

MATERIAL	Single thread white canvas 23 threads to 1″
	Buckram for stiffening. Silk lining
THREAD	Stranded cotton, shades of pink
SIZE	Back 4¾″ x 1¼″. Front 1¼″ x 3¼″
TO MAKE UP	Make the back separately with all turnings invisible. Line the embroidered front piece, also with hidden turnings; place both pieces together and oversew tightly from the outside.

DESIGN TYPE B1

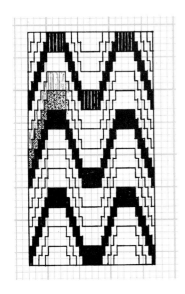

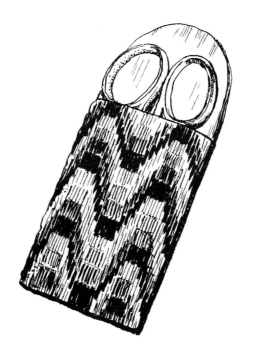

121

NEEDLECASE

MATERIAL	Glenshee Evenweave linen, 28 threads to 1″ Linen lining. Cardboard
THREAD	Stranded cotton
SIZE	Approximately 3″ x 4″. Let this depend on a convenient number of repeats in the design.
TO MAKE UP	Surround the design with a ¼″ band of tent stitch to make a good edge. Work reverse tent stitch down the spine of the book. Hem stitch and fringe several flannel pages or cut with pinking shears. Crease the linen lining straight by the thread; turn down the canvas; place wrong sides together and oversew the two long edges, working from the right side between every thread of the canvas. Sew the hemstitched pages to the spine, catching on to the canvas with invisible stitches. Slip the cardboard into place from each end and close the ends with oversewing.

DESIGN TYPE A3

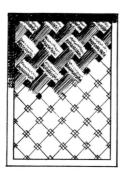

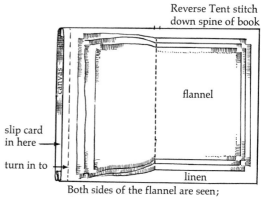

Reverse Tent stitch
down spine of book

canvas

flannel

slip card
in here

turn in to

linen

Both sides of the flannel are seen;
thread ends must be hidden

REVERSE TENT
STITCH
work 4 rows

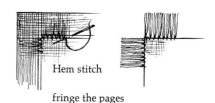

Hem stitch

fringe the pages

TELEPHONE BOOK OR
WRITING CASE COVER

MATERIAL   Single thread canvas, 23 threads to 1″ or Glenshee linen, leaving part of the pattern unworked to incorporate the colour of the fabric in the design.

THREAD   Crewel wool or stranded cotton

It is advisable to have the work mounted professionally on a leather case; therefore a margin of at least 1″ of unworked canvas should be left beyond the design.

DESIGN TYPE D

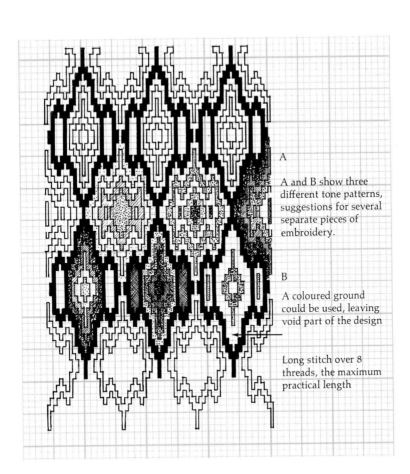

A

A and B show three different tone patterns, suggestions for several separate pieces of embroidery.

B

A coloured ground could be used, leaving void part of the design

Long stitch over 8 threads, the maximum practical length

123

NAPKIN RING

MATERIAL	Single thread white canvas 23 threads to 1″
	Linen lining
THREAD	Stranded cotton
SIZE	2¼″ x 5¾″ circumference
TO MAKE UP	If the pattern at each end is so arranged that it matches perfectly the ring can be joined invisibly. Make the lining slightly smaller; open out the seams, place them face to face; turn in upper and lower edges; oversew the two pieces together, sewing between each thread of the canvas.

DESIGN TYPE A2

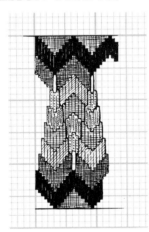

BENCH TOP AND FOOTSTOOL

The bench top could be worked on canvas with exactly the same design as the hand screen on p. 27 or with a wave line adapted from the pattern, or from the line on p. 83 with the number of stitches in each step altered to give a shallower curve.

The motif can be a version of the carnation p. 26; the shell (A), or any other simplified, compact natural form; a small motif (B) based on an A2 pattern p. 78; or (C), adapted from B2, p. 88; or adapted from part of a grounding.

The motif (C) makes use of coloured background fabric to form the centre of the motif, which if used would be seen against the fabric in the space between the wave lines. If this design were used on canvas, the centre would need to be filled in with counted satin stitch, or with tent stitch surrounding the block shown with a dotted line.

The footstool is worked in wool on canvas, and as with the bench, professionally mounted. The pattern in this particular grounding is deceptive, not being exactly square. It would be advisable to begin in the middle and work outwards.

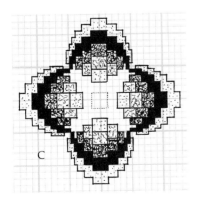

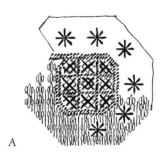

A

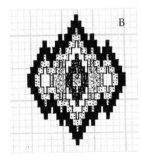

B

C

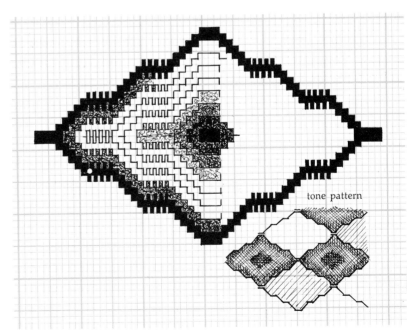

tone pattern

CUSHIONS

A.

MATERIAL — Pale coffee-coloured coarse Glenshee linen, 18 threads to

THREAD — 1″. Stranded cotton (6 strands) and 2 strands of crewel wool.

TO MAKE UP — The design, based on a grounding G7, is enlarged by increasing the number of rows. Motifs are well spaced out to show the background colour.

B.

MATERIAL — Glenshee mercerised cotton fabric, about 19 threads to 1″.

THREAD — A rich cream colour. Stranded cotton (6 strands).

TO MAKE UP — The design, basically the same as that on the hexagonal cushion (p. 128) but with a longer stitch to make sharper points, will need to be drafted on graph paper.

C.

MATERIAL — Yellow Java canvas

THREAD — A heavy wool such as double knitting or Kelim* wool. Anchor soft cotton and 3 strands of crewel wool.

TO MAKE UP — Aida cloth has a distinctive weave which spreads out the embroidery stitches. The scale of this design will depend on thread thickness and on the spacing of rows; there should be at least 7 rows in each band. A fringe of button-hole loops and tassels made of embroidery wool decorates each end. See G7.

D.

MATERIAL — Coloured Glenshee even-weave linen or Willow cross stitch material.

THREAD — 1 or 2 strands of crewel wool and a little Sylko Perlé 5 (Pearl cotton).

A widely spaced design which uses a simple grounding motif. G2

*Not available in the United States but used in England and Europe.

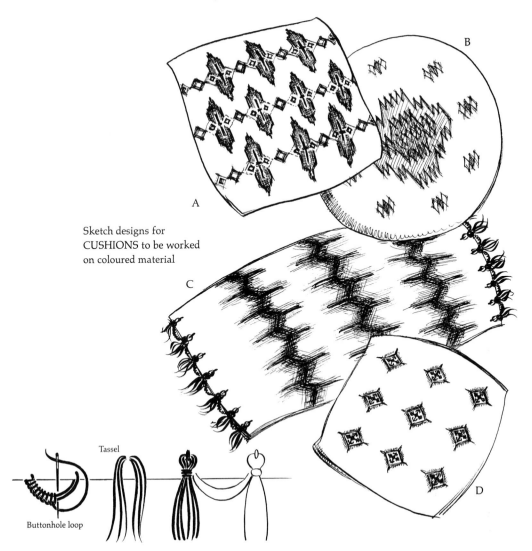

Sketch designs for
CUSHIONS to be worked
on coloured material

A

B

C

D

Tassel

Buttonhole loop

HEXAGONAL CUSHION

MATERIAL	Single weave white canvas, 18 threads to 1″ linen for the back. No. 22 tapestry needles
THREAD	3 ply knitting wool
SIZE	14″ x 18″

This design entails accurate counting. Begin with the outline of the central pattern; work those on either side, then the ones between. After this has been done, the design, wholly in 6.3 step, works out easily. Anchor soft or a very

127

FLORENTINE EMBROIDERY

thick wool can be introduced to make an unusually heavy line, giving further variation to tone and colour.

TO MAKE UP   Rule pencil lines on the canvas to mark the edge. Trim the canvas to about ¾″ from the embroidery and turn under. Turn down the linen straight by the thread and place against the straight thread of the canvas; turn in the diagonal sides with great care not to stretch them out of shape. Tack all round. Oversew on the right side between every wool stitch, at such an angle that the cotton slips between and does not show. Leave one straight edge open until the pad is inserted, then close.

A very fine cord can be added to neaten the edge, but is not essential.

DESIGN TYPE A1

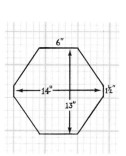

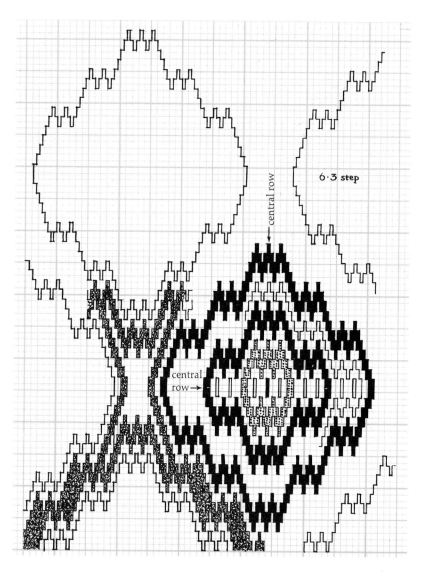

V.

V. ABOVE: Small articles illustrating present-day uses of Florentine embroidery (see pages 121, 124, 135, 136)

BELOW: Sunflower panel
(see page 154, *author's copyright*)

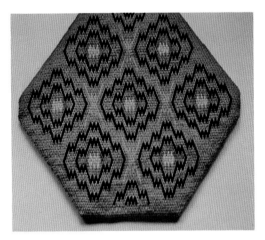

Hexagonal cushion (see page 127)

CUSHION

MATERIAL	Hardanger, 22 pairs of threads to 1″, yellow
THREAD	crewel wool
SIZE	13″ square
METHOD	Work begins with the eyelet; the design develops from the first dark zigzag row of Florentine, 4.2 step. Some yellow fabric remains uncovered to form part of the design. Hardanger material appears to be evenly woven; the difference between warp and weft threads is only slight and has little effect on this design. Two threads of crewel wool are used for the motif and one thread for the Hungarian stitch background texture which is worked throughout with the rows in the same direction.

DESIGN TYPE A2

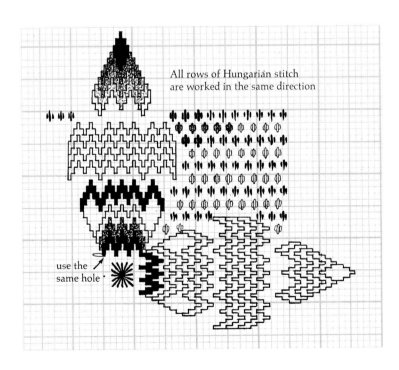

All rows of Hungarian stitch are worked in the same direction

use the same hole

STOOL TOPS

These very simple designs are capable of endless variation. Both can be used in their most obvious form, shading inwards with continuous lines or they can be broken into more elaborate colour arrangements which can be tested on tracing paper laid over the cartoon. Florentine 4.2 step wears better than a longer stitch, but a 6.3 step could be used and further changes made in the number of stitches in the outline. In each diagram the outline is slightly different, showing how easily the design will adapt to fill a given area, such as a stool top which needs re-upholstering.

DESIGN TYPE B2

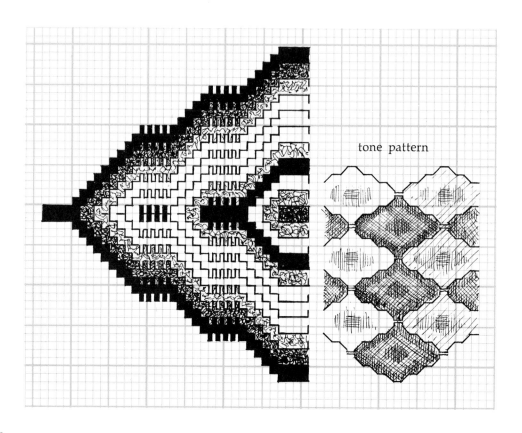

tone pattern

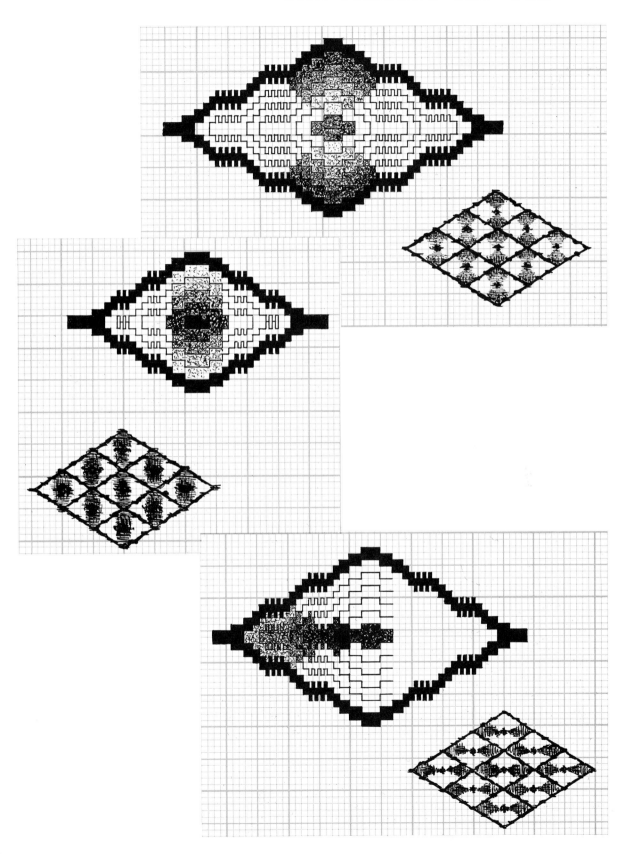

DRESSING STOOL

Both sketches are based on a B I (p. 84) line and are the same except that they are worked with the long edge in the opposite direction. Many shading variations are possible, and provided a limited colour range is chosen, this design will allow fairly strong tone contrasts without becoming garish. An 18 thread to 1″ canvas can be used, with 3 ply knitting wool, tapestry wool or two strands of crewel wool. The work should be mounted professionally.

DESIGN TYPE B1

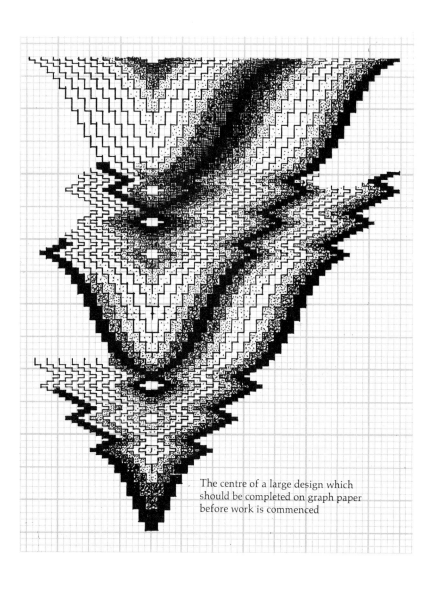

The centre of a large design which should be completed on graph paper before work is commenced

BAGS

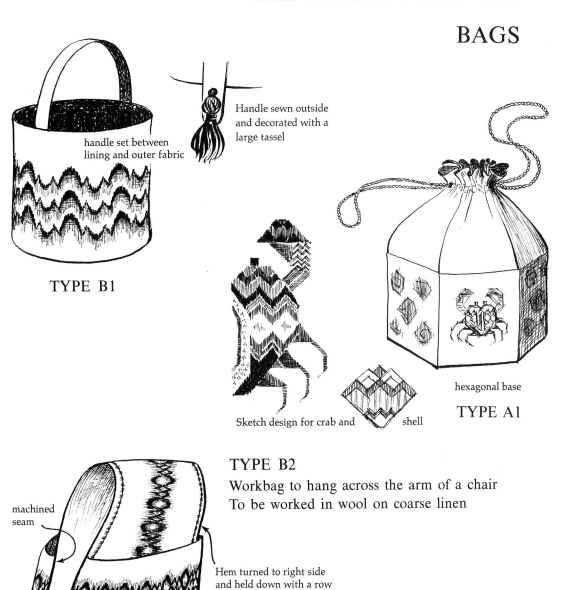

handle set between
lining and outer fabric

Handle sewn outside
and decorated with a
large tassel

TYPE B1

Sketch design for crab and   shell

hexagonal base

TYPE A1

TYPE B2
Workbag to hang across the arm of a chair
To be worked in wool on coarse linen

machined
seam

Hem turned to right side
and held down with a
row of satin stitch;

use 2 shades of wool

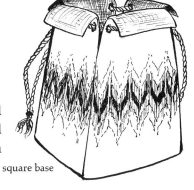

TYPE C
Bag made with 4 separate pieces, machined
together after embroidery completed; lined
with linen to match either the coarse linen
ground or a shade of wool

square base

FLORENTINE EMBROIDERY

BAGS TO BE
PROFESSIONALLY MOUNTED

All three bags should be worked with crewel wool or stranded cotton, on the finest French canvas available, 24 or preferably 28 threads to 1″, or on Glenshee evenweave linen 28 threads to 1″, if a slightly softer material is preferred. Short stitches are most practical, with an absolute maximum of 8 threads. Designs need to be small and compact, with a frequent enough repeat to build up a satisfactory area of patterned fabric.

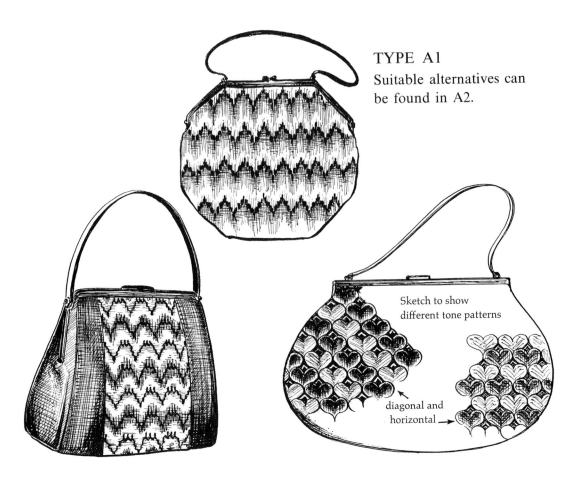

TYPE A1
Suitable alternatives can
be found in A2.

Sketch to show
different tone patterns

diagonal and
horizontal

TYPE E3
Worked in Hungarian point

TYPE B2
With the motif reversed

SCUFFS

MATERIAL	Single thread white canvas, 23 threads to 1″ Wadding for extra softness over slipper soles Cotton lining. Bias binding
THREAD	Crewel wool, dark and mid brown, fawn, blue and pale pink
TO MAKE UP	Sew the bias binding all round the under edge of the sole; pad the upper surface and tack the lining in place leaving a space on either side of the tread for the embroidered band to be inserted. Line the band, pin in position and if possible, test across the foot to ensure a firm grip. When the band is in place between lining and sole, secure one side, then fasten the other which is far less easy to do, (a long darning needle helps to negotiate an awkward piece of sewing). Finally bring the binding level with the top edge of the sole and oversew all round with very small stitches.

DESIGN TYPE B2

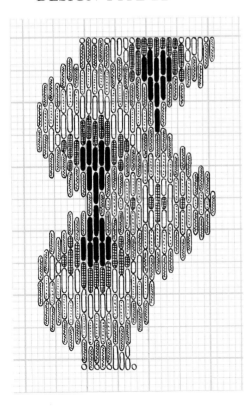

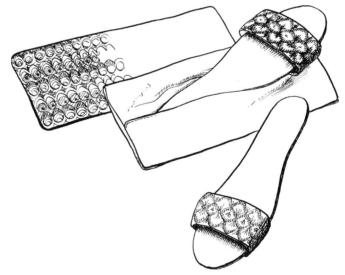

135

SLIPPER OR GLOVE CASE

MATERIAL	Single thread white canvas, 23 threads to 1″ or Glenshee embroidery fabric 18 threads to 1″, a firm but softer material than canvas
	Brown corded cotton lining
THREAD	Crewel wool, shades of yellow, blue, blue-green, greyish-brown, grey
SIZE	4¼″ x 10¾″
TO MAKE UP	Trim the canvas to within about ¼″ of the embroidery, turn under and catch back. Oversew the embroidered panel on to the lining. Neaten both long edges; overlap as if making a pillow case, and machine the two short seams.

DESIGN TYPE B2

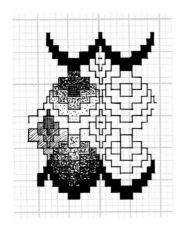

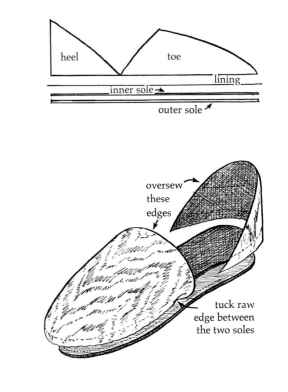

136

SLIPPERS

MATERIAL   Single thread canvas, 20 threads to 1″
                    Stiffening, wadding, cotton lining, soles

THREAD   Crewel wool

TO MAKE UP   Pad, stiffen and line the heel piece, oversewing the curved seam from the right side; leave the lower edge free. Pad the toe piece. Oversew from the right side the curved instep edge, leaving the long curve tacked. Heel and toe must be attached between the bottom of the sole and its lining. On a lamb's-wool sole the edge can be prized up and the slipper pieces eased underneath, tacked, then sewn firmly in place. If separate soles are used, line the inner sole, paste down the edges of the lining to the sole and pin to the outer sole at the instep before sewing heel and toe in place.

DESIGN TYPE E4

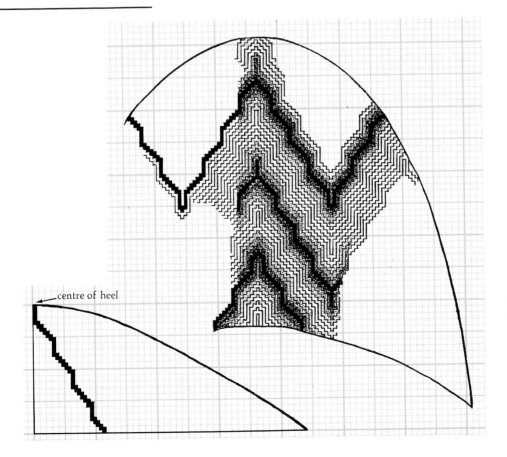

centre of heel

137

GLASSES' CASE

MATERIAL	Single thread canvas, 23 threads to 1″
	Stiffening; either linen or corded silk lining
THREAD	Stranded cotton
SIZE	About 3″ x 6½″
TO MAKE UP	Cover two pieces of stiffening material with the lining by pasting down the edges. Place right sides together and oversew all round except for the opening. Turn down the canvas edges. Place wrong sides together and oversew with large shallow "tacks" to hold the two sides lightly in place. Slip the lining inside. Use a paper knife to slip along inside to make certain that the canvas turning lies flat. Tack the open end to prevent the lining from sliding out. Oversew the two pieces of canvas together, between every embroidery stitch. It is much easier to insert the lining before the canvas is tightly sewn. Finally close both seams at the open end.

GROUNDINGS are most suitable

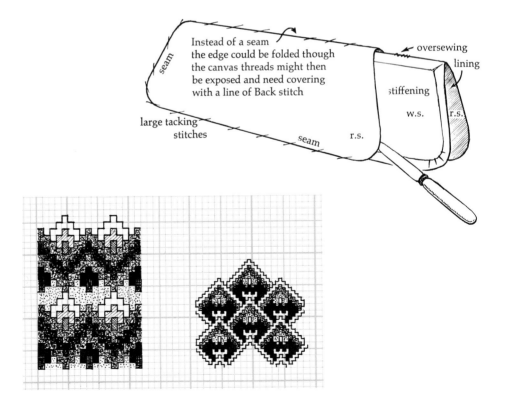

STOOL TOP

MATERIAL   Aida canvas, green fabric only partly covered with embroidery
THREAD   Tapestry wool in shades of green and grey

A complete cartoon need not be drawn; a sketch gives sufficient guidance and allows for ideas to evolve from the stitches as work progresses. Very little counting is needed when the pattern keeps to the same step, Florentine 4.2, and a few other stitches such as Hungarian and star stitch. This diagram shows that unless tones are carefully considered an abstract design can quickly become disjointed. Those areas of material not covered by stitches must balance one another.

STOLE

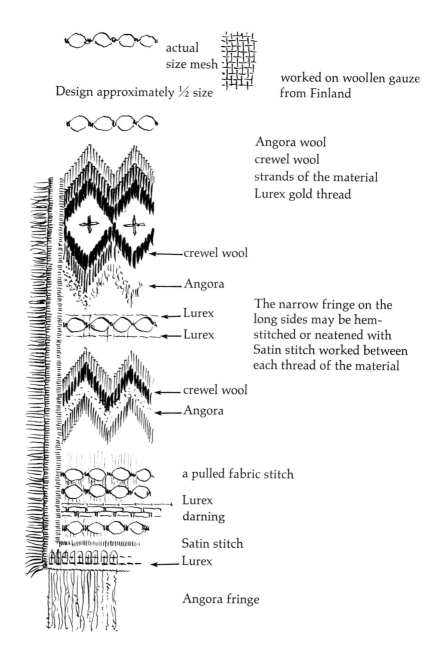

actual
size mesh

Design approximately ½ size

worked on woollen gauze
from Finland

Angora wool
crewel wool
strands of the material
Lurex gold thread

crewel wool

Angora

Lurex

Lurex

The narrow fringe on the
long sides may be hem-
stitched or neatened with
Satin stitch worked between
each thread of the material

crewel wool

Angora

a pulled fabric stitch

Lurex
darning

Satin stitch
Lurex

Angora fringe

140

If fine flannel, red, white, pale grey or natural, with a fairly loose weave is substituted for the woollen gauze, drawn thread work must take the place of pulled fabric work

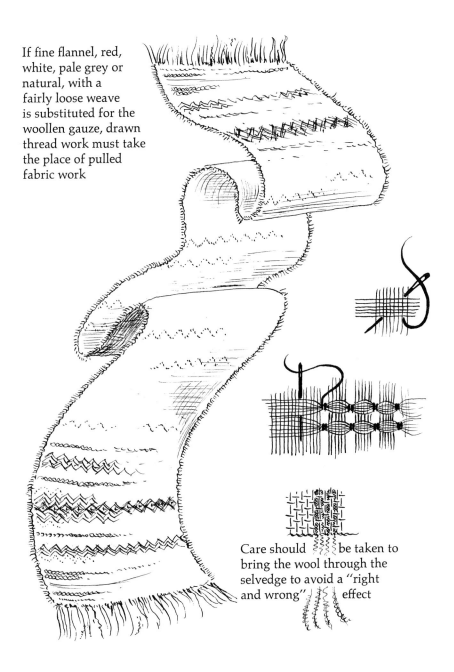

Care should be taken to bring the wool through the selvedge to avoid a "right and wrong" effect

141

VANITY BAG

MATERIAL	Willow cross stitch fabric, grey
	Linen lining, green
	Transparent plastic sheeting
	6″ zip fastener. Pearl and bronze beads
THREAD	Stranded cotton, stone, grey, lime green, white
	Sylko perlé, No 5 (Pearl cotton), stone
SIZE	$6\frac{1}{2}$″ x $4\frac{1}{4}$″
TO MAKE UP	Tack a guide line to indicate finished size. Do not cut the material to shape until the embroidery is finished. The first complete line of stitches is worked far enough from the top edge to allow room for the adjusted line (see diag.) to be added when the rest of the embroidery is finished. Several rows at the bottom also need adjustment at each end, to fit to the curve of the bag. When completed, place face downwards on a soft surface, press, ironing outwards from the centre. Do not damp. Sew on the beads. Cut the fabric to shape, tack the side seams straight by the thread and machine them. Machine green linen and plastic lining together, making them very slightly smaller to fit inside the bag. One edge of the zip can be machined between lining and outer fabric, the other edge must be finished by hand. Great care must be taken to set the zip in straight. Make a small tassel from embroidery thread to finish the zip tag.

DESIGN TYPE C

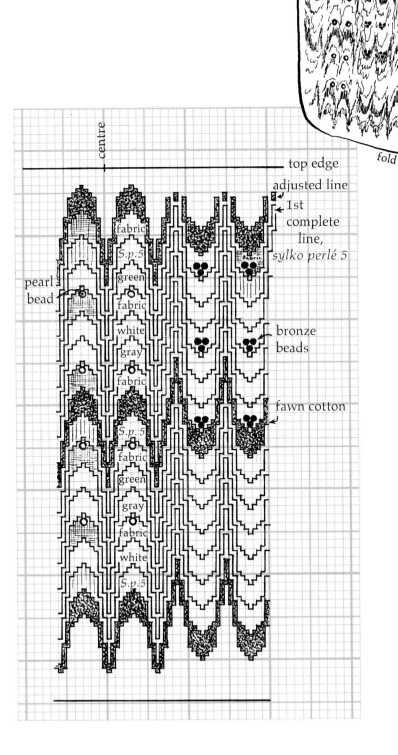

centre

top edge

adjusted line

1st
complete
line,
sylko perlé 5

fabric

S.p.5

green

fabric

pearl
bead

white

gray

bronze
beads

fabric

fawn cotton

S.p.5

fabric

green

gray

fabric

white

S.p.5

fold

seam
ends here

143

CHILD'S APRON

MATERIAL	Willow even-weave, white
THREAD	Stranded cotton, pink, cerise, blue, green
	4 strands used for embroidery
	Hemstitching worked with one strand of the fabric
TO MAKE UP	To prevent fraying while work is in progress, turn under and tack hems at a distance from the final edge. When the embroidery is finished, count threads on either side and see that each hem has the same number of threads when turned under. On coarse material even one extra thread makes a noticeable difference to the width. Turn up the bottom hem straight by the thread. Cut away a small piece at each end to make the corners lie flat. Remove one thread and work handkerchief hemstitch. Embroider the band with satin stitch and star stitches; make up the ties, hemming into each thread of the fabric. This method is easier than turning inside out when the band is narrow or the fabric frays. Having made small pleats at the top of the apron, set it into the band, tacking into place by the thread to keep it straight and finally hemming along the back.

DESIGN TYPE B1

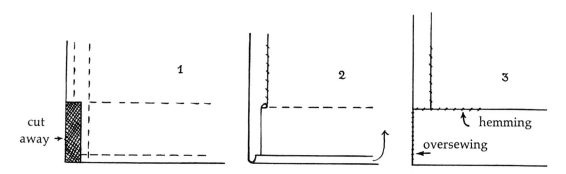

How to turn a corner with different width hems

VI. Decorative panels showing the adaptability of Florentine patterns to modern designs (see pages 148-151; fish and owl, *author's copyright*)

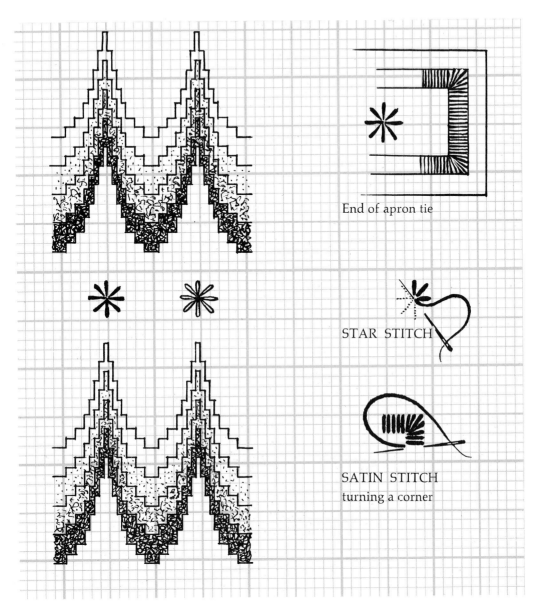

End of apron tie

STAR STITCH

SATIN STITCH
turning a corner

See page 72 for picture of apron.

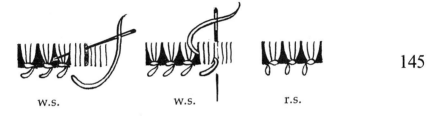

w.s.   w.s.   r.s.

Hem stitch

145

BELL PULL AND TIE BACK
FOR DRAPERY

To be worked in wool or stranded cotton and a little Sylko
Perlé on canvas

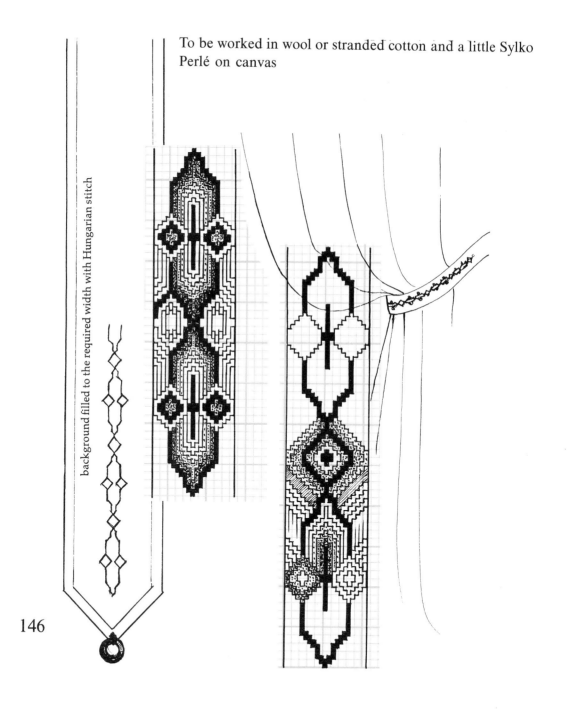

background filled to the required width with Hungarian stitch

146

DECORATIVE PANELS

To be worked on coloured even-weave material in various threads, or on red flannel in different thicknesses of white thread and a little very dark red

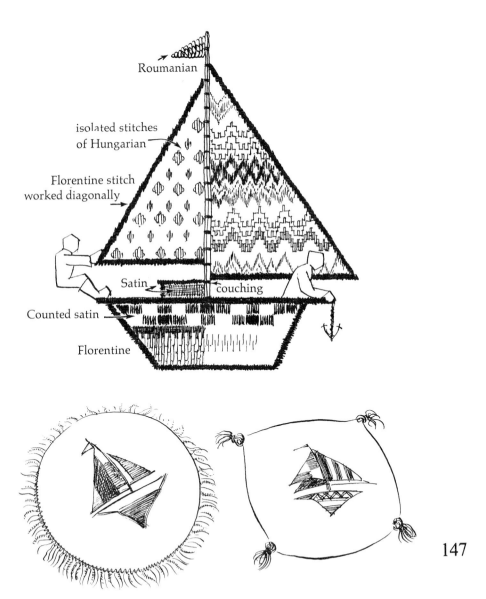

Roumanian

isolated stitches of Hungarian

Florentine stitch worked diagonally

Satin

couching

Counted satin

Florentine

147

DECORATIVE PANELS · SHIPS

A series of small panels to hang beside a child's bed

DECORATIVE PANELS · SHIPS

Patterns used to cover
the background.
Diagrams to show the transition

from zigzag to curve

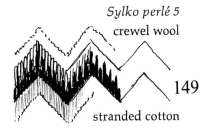

Sylko perlé 5
crewel wool

149

stranded cotton

DECORATIVE PANEL · FISH

Design development,
first sketch and
stitch suggestions
(AUTHOR'S COPYRIGHT)

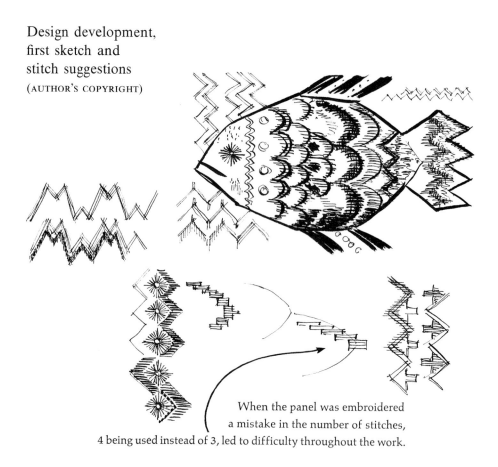

When the panel was embroidered
a mistake in the number of stitches,
4 being used instead of 3, led to difficulty throughout the work.

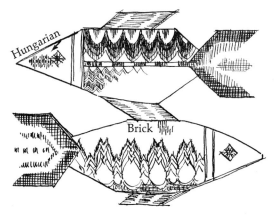

150

Sketch for a panel or cushion
to be worked on even-weave
linen, royal blue or jade,
25 threads to 1″

DECORATIVE PANELS · OWL

Embroidered on Norland openweave linen in crewel wool, stranded cotton and threads of the material itself. Lines of pulled fabric work make a light background texture. The loose weave of the fabric helped to create the pattern on the breast. The wings in Florentine stitch 6.2 step are worked in diagonal rows, a speedy method used on some Italian 17th century bedcovers. (AUTHOR'S COPYRIGHT)

Student's sketch in strong black outline and water-colour. Curves became straight lines when translated into stitches.

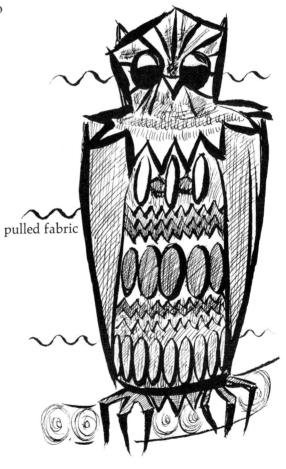

pulled fabric

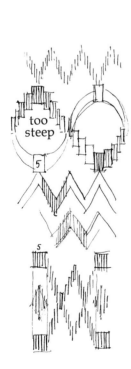

Eventual alteration in wing shape has not improved upon the original idea.

DECORATIVE PANEL · ROOSTER

Design notes from a student's sketch book

DECORATIVE PANEL · BISON

Prehistoric painting which inspired a design on canvas

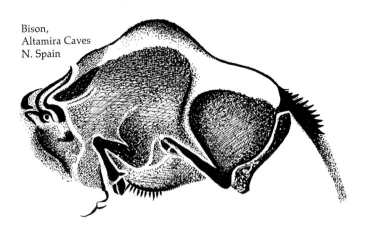

Bison,
Altamira Caves
N. Spain

A student's interpretation of a similar Altamira bison; the work was carried
out mainly in shades of bronze, golden brown, olive green and grey.

Framed panel

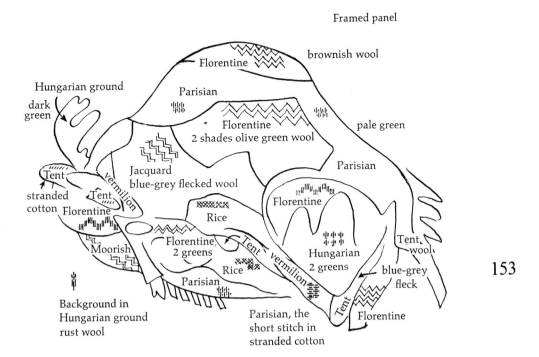

brownish wool

Florentine

Hungarian ground
dark
green

Parisian

Florentine
2 shades olive green wool

pale green

Parisian

Jacquard
blue-grey flecked wool

Florentine

Tent

vermilion

stranded
cotton   Tent
Florentine

Rice

Moorish

Florentine
2 greens

Tent   vermilion

Hungarian
2 greens

Tent wool

Rice

blue-grey
fleck

Parisian

Tent

Florentine

Background in
Hungarian ground
rust wool

Parisian, the
short stitch in
stranded cotton

153

SUNFLOWER

Sunflower, 10″ x 9″, worked in shades of lime green, greenish yellow, gold, orange and red crewel wool on lemon yellow linen scrim, embellished with pearl dewdrops and viridian, green, bronze, gunmetal and jet faceted beads (AUTHOR'S COPYRIGHT)

THE PLACE OF FLORENTINE EMBROIDERY IN ECCLESIASTICAL WORK

Ecclesiastical work is a specialised branch of embroidery, in which Florentine stitch and Hungarian point can have only a limited use because, on the whole, the patterns produced tend to be dominating. If, however, they are chosen with discretion, having due regard for suitability of scale and colour, more handsome work could be done today than in 17th century Italy when numerous vestments and altar frontals were made. Florentine embroidery has proved its adaptability and could with care combine with symbolic designs and the traditional colours of the church to decorate the following articles:—

Alms or collecting bags
Altar frontals
Banners (if used among other stitches)
Communion rail kneelers
Cushions, (as a book rest or missal stand for pulpit or altar)
Door curtains
Kneeling pads (without gusset)
Kneelers or hassocks (with gusset)
Lectern falls
Sanctuary hassocks (usually several inches deeper than kneelers)

APPENDIX I
Historical Examples of Florentine Embroidery

Boston Museum of Fine Arts: various examples of domestic work, vestments
Boughton House, Northamptonshire: bench cover, chair upholstery, stools
Cooper Union Museum, New York: purses, chasuble, burse
Deerfield, Massachusetts: bag, bed curtains and valances, bell pull, carpet, chair upholstery,
   lace maker's box, purses, wallet
Drayton House, Northamptonshire: bed curtains and valances, chair upholstery
Glasgow, City Museum and Art Gallery: samplers
Florence, The Bargello: chair upholstery
Jewish Museum, London: Ark curtains
The Metropolitan Museum of Art, New York: miscellaneous fragments and panels, altar
   frontal, fragment with Hebrew inscription, samplers
Parham Park, Sussex: bed curtains and valances, cover for bed or table
Shelburne, Vermont: chair upholstery, window draperies and valances
The Victoria and Albert Museum, London: chair upholstery, cover for bed or table, handscreen,
   miscellaneous fragments and panels, pincushion, shoes, altar frontal, Ark curtains, samplers,
   Hatton Garden hangings (Hungarian stitch in company with other shading stitches)
Colonial Williamsburg, Virginia: bedspread, chair upholstery, daybed, lace maker's box,
   panels, pocket books, toilet box

APPENDIX II
Embroidery at Boughton House, Kettering

1. A set of William and Mary open armchairs, the moulded arms terminating in scrolls on
turned supports, legs and stretchers, with ball feet, the seats and high rectangular backs
stuffed and covered in Flame pattern needlework.

A walnut open armchair, almost en suite, similarly upholstered.

A pair of William and Mary walnut stools, on moulded S-scroll legs united by waved
H-shaped stretchers, the rectangular tops similarly upholstered.

A Charles II walnut long stool, with eight spirally turned legs on stretchers, the top
inset with canework panel and loose squab seat similarly covered in Flame pattern needlework, 66½″ long.

A Georgian mahogany settee, on square legs united by plain stretchers, the high
rectangular back, scroll arms and squab seat in three sections stuffed and covered with
similar needlework, 75″ wide.

156   These pieces are not all of the same date although all are now covered in the same

needlework, so that the needlework is unlikely to have been the original covering. It is regarded as being roughly of the William and Mary period or of only slightly later date.

2. The great State bed which belonged to Boughton is now in the Victoria and Albert Museum, complete with its hangings of Italian crimson brocade. The bed from which the needlework now covering the gilt legged furniture in the Fifth state room came was only a Victorian four-poster. The needlework was in straight strips, not apparently designed as bed-hangings, but used for that purpose. It was much older than the bed and is believed to be English workmanship, most probably of the William and Mary period or possibly Charles II, since that is the time when this kind of possession was being acquired by the Montagues. It is very likely to have been contemporary with the Drayton bed. This furniture is officially described as follows:

A giltwood winged settee, a pair of winged chairs and two stools, the turned and tapering legs with vertical fluting and beading, developed into inverted-cup feet, the legs united by moulded X-shaped stretchers, entirely upholstered in contemporary needlework in colours, with bold scrolling foliage, vases and flower sprays with strapwork bands, on a cream ground, late 17th century, (Boughton believes William and Mary), the settee 55½″ wide, the stools 20¾″ wide.

The carpenter who dismantled the Victorian bed from which this needlework was taken says that it was the usual Victorian four-poster, less than 100 years old, and that the panel filling in the posts at the bedhead was made up of three panels of the embroideries, stitched together vertically; there were two hangings, one at each side of the bedhead, each about the width of the pillow; a straight flat strip of similar embroidery ran round the tester and the bottom valance consisted of a similar straight flat strip perhaps 18″ deep. There is no record of any matching coverlet. He thinks, though he is only guessing, that these hangings had been transferred from an earlier bed, and this seems likely, for a good deal of Montague property was sent to Boughton from time to time from Montague House in London. No more pieces of this embroidery have been found in any of the present houses, but there are scraps which were left over when the hangings were converted to chair covers, including a great deal of narrow decorative border in stump work which seems to have been contemporary with the embroideries and was used with the hangings on the Victorian bed. The embroidery is of excellent quality, in design, colour and workmanship and must originally have dressed a bed of considerable importance.

For this detailed information I am grateful to Her Grace The Duchess of Buccleuch and Miss A. L. Kinnison.

BIBLIOGRAPHY

DEAN, BERYL, *Ecclesiastical Embroidery*. London: B. T. Batsford Ltd., 1958

* GRAY, JENNIFER, *Canvas Embroidery*. London: B. T. Batsford Ltd., 1960

SCHUETTE, MARIE, and MÜLLER-CHRISTENSEN, SIGRID, *The Art of Embroidery*, text translated by King, Donald. London: Thames and Hudson 1964; (original edition Ernst Wasmuth Tubingen, Germany 1963)

SNOOK, BARBARA L., *Learning to Embroider*. London: B. T. Batsford Ltd., 1960

SNOOK, BARBARA L., *Embroidery Stitches*. London: B. T. Batsford Ltd., 1963

SNOOK, BARBARA L., *Needlework Stitches*. New York: Crown Pub. Inc., 1963

* THESIGER, ERNEST, *Adventures in Embroidery*. London: Studio, 1941

* *Antico Lavoro Fiorentino*. Florence: Ortolani & Co., 1925

* Out of Print

158

STITCHES